LEAN SIX SIGMA

QuickStart Guide

SECOND EDITION

The Simplified Beginner's Guide to Lean Six Sigma

Benjamin Sweeney

in partnership with

Edition #2: Created January 4, 2017

Cover Illustration and Design: Katie Poorman, Copyright © 2016 by ClydeBank Media LLC
Interior Design: Katie Poorman, Copyright © 2016 by ClydeBank Media LLC
Editors: Marilyn Burkley & Bryan Basamanowicz

All Rights Reserved

Printed in the United States of America

Publisher's Cataloging-In-Publication Data
(Prepared by The Donohue Group, Inc.)

Names: Sweeney, Benjamin. | ClydeBank Business.
Title: Lean Six Sigma quickstart guide : the simplified beginner's guide to Lean Six Sigma / Benjamin Sweeney,
in partnership with ClydeBank Business.
Description: Second edition. | Albany, NY : ClydeBank Media, LLC, 2016. | Includes bibliographical references.
Identifiers: LCCN 2016962417 | ISBN 978-1-945051-14-2 | ISBN 978-1-945051-24-1 (ebook)
Subjects: LCSH: Six sigma (Quality control standard) | Lean manufacturing. | Industrial efficiency--Management.
Classification: LCC TS156 .S94 2016 (print) | LCC TS156 (ebook) | DDC 658.4013--dc23

ClydeBank Media LLC
P.O. Box 6561
Albany, NY 12206

www.clydebankmedia.com

ISBN-13 : 978-1-945051-14-2

contents

BEFORE YOU START READING, DOWNLOAD YOUR FREE DIGITAL ASSETS!

Be sure to visit the URL below on your computer or mobile device to access the free digital asset files that are included with your purchase of this book.

These digital assets will compliment the material in the book and are referenced throughout the text.

DOWNLOAD YOURS HERE:

www.clydebankmedia.com/leansix-assets

introduction

In the ever-changing business market, one thing is certain: organizations that want to survive must find their own source of competitive edge. One way to secure a lasting advantage is through the optimization of business functions and processes. This is certainly an "easier said than done" scenario, and as the organization grows, the more daunting the challenge appears. Decision makers are nearly inundated with the variety of business improvement methods, optimization programs, and best practice solutions that exist in today's market.

This book introduces readers to the hybrid solution Lean Six Sigma—its constituent elements, how it operates, what tools are available to organizations that utilize Lean Six Sigma, and what criticisms of the program exist.

Lean Six Sigma is born out of a combination of the best parts of both the Japanese automobile manufacturer Toyota's Lean production system and Motorola's quality control program, Six Sigma. As we will see, each program offers significant merits in its own right, and each contributes to the hybrid system's effectiveness and implementation.

However, there are no one-size-fits-all solutions for every organization; the right decision for any business is an informed one. This is a key part of understanding each of the options and methods that are available and how they interact with an organization's operations and structure.

Lean and Six Sigma are both derived from the production and manufacturing sector, but both programs have applications outside the industry of their origin. Lean's focus on detecting and eliminating waste has applications throughout many types of business operations and a variety of industries. Six Sigma's customer-centric quality improvement programs can be applied to many quantifiable business processes in the service industry as well as its home industrial sector.

How to Use This Book

This book has a progressive structure. Lean Six Sigma is a hybrid system of management, and the text therefore begins with descriptions of the two component systems before diving into an analysis of Lean Six Sigma itself.

The chapters that follow describe how the system has been utilized in the manufacturing sector and where it originated, as well as explorations of other industries where the method may be used to substantial effect. Methods, tools, and best practices are all included within this text, as well as a structured examination of the ways in which the elements of Lean Six Sigma can be used to improve an organization's quality, efficiency, and complexity.

Criticism of Lean Six Sigma is discussed in its own chapter. The final chapter, which discusses the Lean Six Sigma consultation industry, highlights the salient questions surrounding the use of outside management experts. The purpose of this book is to provide basic introductory insight into Lean Six Sigma and its real-world implementation for professionals and students alike.

| 1 |

An Introduction to Six Sigma

In This Chapter

- An overview of the Six Sigma method is covered
- An exploration of the concept of standard deviation and its relevance to Six Sigma is explained
- The core methods of DMAIC & DMADV are illustrated
- Staff implications and the Six Sigma organizational hierarchy are discussed

Six Sigma is a quality improvement oriented process management system. It uses statistical tools and empirical techniques to reduce the number of defects within a process to a miniscule level. Developed by the multinational telecommunications company Motorola in 1986, it has evolved into a process-focused business strategy and manufacturing tool that promises highly sought-after results.

In 2005, nineteen years after the conception and adoption of Six Sigma, Motorola claimed to have saved over $17 billion thanks to their adherence to Six Sigma. The continued adoption and implementation of the program—now thirty years old—by Fortune 500 companies and global market players demonstrates its efficacy and staying power as a business improvement tool. In 2011 the International Organization for Standardization (ISO) cemented Six Sigma as a business improvement process with the "13053:2011 ISO" standardized definition.

Like many quality improvement strategies, the exact practical implementation of Six Sigma varies from industry to industry and product to product, but the entire program is shaped around a doctrine of several guiding precepts. Many of these defining principles are evident in traditional quality improvement programs as well, and the program of Six Sigma methodologies is also derived from this venerated framework.

Note that the umbrella term "process" is used here and elsewhere in this text. While Six Sigma was introduced as a *manufacturing* process improvement tool, it is applicable to nearly all quantifiable business processes. The most notable of these non-manufacturing quantifiable processes are the fields of billing and call center or support center efficiency control. The ubiquity of these business activities means that Six Sigma has the potential to spread to all corners of the business world, at least in some capacity.

Core Doctrine

The core doctrines that guide the Six Sigma program can be represented by three key elements. These elements are broad-strokes concepts that serve to inform both adherents to the methodology and those seeking to understand it at its most basic levels.

fig. 1

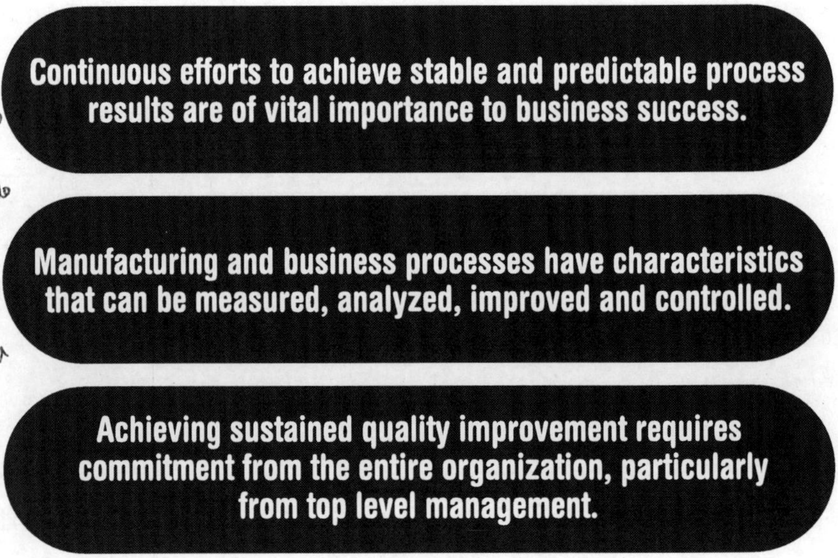

Cont process

Measurable and Changeble

Continuous efforts to achieve stable and predictable process results are of vital importance to business success.

Manufacturing and business processes have characteristics that can be measured, analyzed, improved and controlled.

Commitment

Achieving sustained quality improvement requires commitment from the entire organization, particularly from top level management.

The first portion of the Six Sigma core doctrine represents the ① general aim of most quality improvement programs: the reduction of variation, resulting in increased quality. In the world of Six Sigma manufacturing, the type of variation most often addressed is the defect rate, measured as the defects per million opportunities *(DPMO)*.

Defects incur costs, and costs affect profits. A common aim of the Six Sigma program is to achieve what is known as "Six Sigma quality," a term that refers to processes that produce a defect rate less than or equal to 3.4 DPMO.

To put that in perspective, that same defect rate expressed as a percentage means that defects will occur .00034 percent of the time. However, this proportion does not necessarily represent the number of defects that a process can allow under the Six Sigma approach; the exact allowable percentage should be determined by quality control experts and resource planning personnel within each business unit that implements Six Sigma on a product-by-product basis.

Because the term comes up frequently, it is important to define what a *defect* is. In the Six Sigma process, defects are unwanted variations in the manufacturing process that fall outside of the customer's specifications. This is an extremely broad definition and intentionally so. Defects are commonly thought of as errors such as drilling a bowling ball with two holes instead of three, but the Six Sigma definition also includes non-production aspects that fail to meet the customer's expectations, such as late delivery.

The multitude of different products and production processes use a large variety of methods, tools, and machines to meet customers' needs. The production of claw hammers, for example, requires an entirely different set of materials and machines than does the production of laptop computers. The term "defect" is broad because if the tolerance for the diameter of the hammer's head is 1 ± .05 cm, and three hammers are produced with head diameters of 1.02, 1.04, and .98 cm, then no defects have occurred. But if that same variation existed within the laptop manufacturing process with a tighter tolerance of 1 ± .001, then that spread would be entirely defective. These examples would be considered production defects.

The definition of a defect can also apply to other non-production business processes. Failure to fulfill on-time delivery, for example, is a defect in the sense that what was provided to the customer was outside their specifications—late delivery. Exceeding stated budgets can also be a defect not related to the production process, but certainly is outside of the customer's expectations.

The second Six Sigma doctrine component describes how and where the program is applicable. As a statistical and quantitative process, it is ideal for repetitive processes that can be measured. The definition of an appropriate process for Six Sigma application also establishes the definition of a process for which Six Sigma is *not* ideal.

Unit production, the design process, a service process, billing and data retrieval—these processes are all quantifiable. The creative process, however, is not. Brainstorming, product conceptualization, and pre-design through post-design phases all defy quantification and therefore are very poor candidates for the Six Sigma approach. Also, as outlined later in this text, the need for specialized coaching and training often makes small organizations or low-volume processes poor candidates for extensive Six Sigma applications, as the cost of training and implementation can be exhaustive of resources.

The third principle of Six Sigma is the broadest element of the core doctrine. Change that is imposed upon corporate culture requires support from all levels of the organization, and Six Sigma is no exception. A top-to-bottom implementation of new methodology cannot permeate an enterprise without unanimous consent.

Based on these three pillars, additional doctrine elements are defined that reflect the statistical and targeted nature of Six Sigma.

Six Sigma adoption hinges on the following additional characteristics:

- A clear focus on achieving measurable and quantifiable financial returns from any Six Sigma project
- An increased emphasis on strong and passionate management leadership and support
- A special infrastructure of program-specific staff ranks and hierarchy to lead and implement the Six Sigma approach
- A clear commitment to making decisions on the basis of verifiable data and statistical methods rather than assumptions and guesswork

With these additional doctrine elements, the focus narrows from a broad progress measurement program and quality-focused implementation, to the top-to-bottom process management system that Six Sigma represents. The first point reflects the purpose of adopting Six Sigma: improvement. It is no surprise that a statistically-based system defines improvement as measurable and quantifiable.

The second point reflects the necessary commitment to effect change within a large organization. Strong leadership and total commitment to the Six Sigma approach, like any paradigm shift in corporate culture, helps ensure that the goals of the program are realized and that any positive change is lasting.

There is no stronger supporter of Six Sigma's effectiveness in a multinational conglomerate than Jack Welch, former CEO of General Electric (GE). Welch implemented Six Sigma at GE in 1995 and adopted it straight from the source: Motorola. In his 2005 book entitled *Winning*, he states, "Nothing compares to the effectiveness of Six Sigma when it comes to improving a company's operational efficiency, raising its productivity, and lowering its costs." Even after Welch's departure from GE, the company still utilizes the Six Sigma approach.

The third point reflects program-specific terminology and implications for staff. A *"colored belt system"* that denotes trainers, implementers, and rank-and-file employees is devised to provide a skeleton around which the Six Sigma program is built. Staff implications are covered in more detail later within this chapter.

The fourth point reflects the program's statistical nature and the assertion that the strength of Six Sigma lies in data. The appropriate use of data modeling, benchmarking, and other statistical methods is considered the foundation of the Six Sigma approach, and this aspect of the doctrine serves to codify that fact.

Even the program's name, "Six Sigma," is a reflection of the statistical methods that the program utilizes. In the world of statistics, a lower case sigma, the eighteenth letter of the Greek alphabet (written as σ), represents the *standard deviation*, or the average distribution of variation within a data set.

The lower the standard deviation, the closer the data points are to the average; the higher the standard deviation, the farther away the data points are from the average. A reduction in variance aims for a lower standard deviation or a number that is closer to the average for the data set. While the program's name is often spelled out, it may also be referred to simply as 6σ.

The term "Six Sigma" stems from the original specifications that Motorola laid out with the maiden implementation of the program. This specification outlined the maximum difference from average data, or "deviance," that was allowed. Standard deviation is, statistically speaking, a form of variance within a data set. Practically speaking, this is the number of units that conform to the allotted specifications.

Again, statistically speaking, variance is defined as the average of the squares of the distance each value is from the *mean* (average) value. This may seem daunting, and statistical quantification can become quite complex, but for the purposes of an introduction to the Lean Six Sigma program, a simple summary of the concepts behind standard deviation follows. This is the absolute basis of standard deviation calculation and theory, and a practical application of the standard deviation formula is explored within the next chapter.

Standard Deviation & the Story Behind 6σ

Standard deviation is discussed in detail later in this text; this summary is included to explore the roots of the Six Sigma program. Standard deviation is expressed as the following formula:

fig. 2

$$\sigma = \sqrt{\frac{\Sigma\,(X - \overline{X})^2}{n}}$$

Where

x = each value within the data set

$\overline{x}$ = the mean or arithmetical average

n = the number of values in the data set

Note : Readers may recognize an upper case sigma (Σ) as the summation symbol, or the statistical operation that produces a sum of a column or group of numbers. Here it serves the same function as the addition operator within the equation.

This formula is applied to each value for x within the data set, which determines a final σ value. The specific tolerances for a process determine which values for σ are acceptable DPMO rates and which are considered outside tolerance for the process.

Within data that has a normal distribution, pictured below as a normal distribution graph, the mean (average), *median* (midpoint of the data), and *mode* (most often occurring value) are all located at the center of the graph. The curve is smooth and symmetric on either side. The curve never touches the x-axis as it slopes away from the center—although it may appear to due to scale—but gets increasingly closer by a smaller and smaller factor. The total area under the curve is 1.0 or 100 percent. This type of graph is often referred to as a bell curve.

Using the concept of standard deviation and normal distribution, we can shift away from the center of a normal distribution graph in either the positive or negative direction by a distance of σ. In any given set of normally distributed data, a (1σ) in each direction away from the mean will span across approximately 68 percent of the entire data range. A shift of 2σ represents roughly 95 percent of the data. Shift 3σ away from the center and about 99.7 percent of area under the curve is encompassed—or 99.7 percent of the data is included.

fig. 3

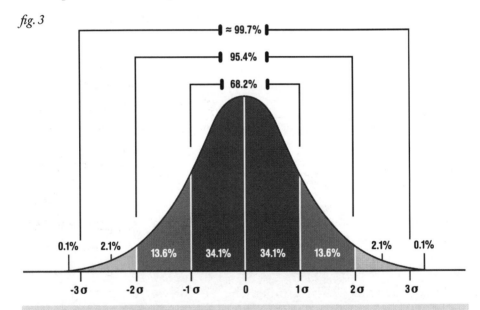

Note : *Even though the curve never touches the x-axis, the area under it still represents 100 percent, a fact that can be proved mathematically using calculus. An exploration of this proof is well beyond and in an entirely different direction from the scope of this book.*

The term "Six Sigma" then represents the percentage of the area under the normal distribution curve that is 6σ distance (3σ in each direction) from the middle. For practical purposes, this means that the difference between 6 standard deviations and 100 percent is the allowable defect rate (3.4 DPMO).

DMAIC & DMADV

While standard deviation and the sigma shift are effective tools to determine the parameters of a process, they can only tell decision makers what is happening or what should be happening, not how to fix a high defect rate or other issues.

To improve existing processes within a business unit, the Six Sigma program offers the *DMAIC* method (pronounced "duh-may-ick"). DMAIC is an acronym for "Define, Measure, Analyze, Improve, and Control."

fig. 4

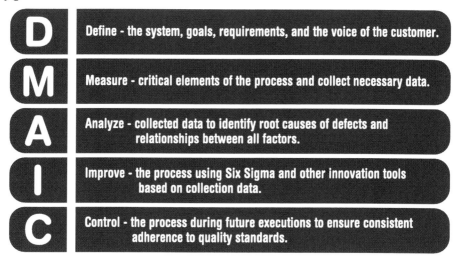

D — Define - the system, goals, requirements, and the voice of the customer.

M — Measure - critical elements of the process and collect necessary data.

A — Analyze - collected data to identify root causes of defects and relationships between all factors.

I — Improve - the process using Six Sigma and other innovation tools based on collection data.

C — Control - the process during future executions to ensure consistent adherence to quality standards.

A variation of this method, oriented toward the introduction of new product lines and processes, is the *DMADV* ("duh-mad-vee") process. This acronym represents the steps "Define, Measure, Analyze, Design, and Verify." The DMADV process is also referred to as Design for Six Sigma (DFSS). Neither the process for improvement nor the process for introduction that Six Sigma offers is isolated to the realm of manufacturing. Most quantifiable business processes can benefit from DMAIC analysis and can be introduced using the DMADV method.

fig. 5

D	**Define** - target goals and the needs of the customer.
M	**Measure** - and identify elements that are Critical to Quality (CTQs).
A	**Analyze** - characteristics that have been defined and measured to determine design alternatives.
D	**Design** - an improved alternative that is a "best fit" based on measurements and analysis.
V	**Verify** - the design and begin implementation of the process.

DMAIC is a common thread throughout the entire Six Sigma program, and the DMAIC method can be seen in nearly every Six Sigma improvement application. DMAIC is a closed loop process that offers a structured approach for process improvement through analysis, observation, and verification. Later in this book we discuss the Lean practice of kaizen, and that methodology's culture of constant incremental improvement, and the fitness of Lean and Six Sigma together as a business improvement program is made increasingly clear as both components are explored.

When undertaking DMAIC activities, the first step is to define all relevant aspects of the task. This includes data to be collected, what goals the DMAIC activities seek to accomplish, and an overall business case for the process.

Measurements are made; measurements represent a key component of improvement. Initial measurements represent benchmarks, or a record of the initial, or in some cases current, state of a process. Once measurements are made again they serve as feedback that can inform decision makers in regard to the success or failure of their improvement efforts. Measuring the process through data collection and observations is the measurement component of the DMAIC process.

Once a suitable body of data has been measured, the results are compiled and analyzed through the lens of the initially defined goals. Decision makers should ask themselves what the data is telling them, and what that translates into as far as customer satisfaction. This represents the analysis component of DMAIC.

If the results are less than favorable, then corrective action should be implemented to effect positive change within the process at hand. This is the improvement component of the DMAIC process.

The process is again measured to verify that the methods implemented have produced results that meet the defined goals. DMAIC is a cyclic process; the final control step entails returning to previous steps within the DMAIC process to produce effective improvement (often referred to as innovation). This could entail revisiting the measurement step and the accuracy or suitability of data collection methods, or even going back to the first stage and redefining the goals of the DMAIC activity.

If improvement efforts are successful, then the learning and insights generated should be shared across the organization where applicable and should be developed into a best practice for future operations. An organization grows and improves as innovation is uncovered and cemented into processes that establish a new and improved baseline for all business activities.

First the data to be collected or goals to be met are defined. The data is collected, observations made, or information recorded (measure). The results are studied for insight and learning (analyze), and then the feedback is put into action (improve). Once the systems are in place, the new learning is codified into process and the improvements are maintained (control).

A key element in both the DMAIC and DMADV methods is an overriding focus on the needs of the customer. Organizations that structure their processes and operations around the needs of the customer realize that customer satisfaction is an inherent attribute of quality and customer retention.

VOC /
TQM

This focus has become known within Six Sigma and beyond as listening to the Voice of the Customer (VOC), an element that is also found in the Lean method, though going by a number of different names. VOC is also an element of an organizational doctrine known as Total Quality Management (TQM).

Total Quality Management is a quality control program that is parallel to Six Sigma and that some readers may be familiar with. TQM identifies and embodies the concept that a high-quality product that has "poor fitness" for the customer's needs is of little value, and value and quality are customer-driven characteristics. TQM was developed as a response to lagging industrial progress in the United States relative to Japan's manufacturing strength in the late 1980s and early '90s. It has since fallen out of the spotlight, overshadowed by programs such as ISO 9000, Lean, and Six Sigma, which have gained popularity over the past few decades.

In addition to the DMAIC and DMADV methods, Six Sigma utilizes a bevy of statistical and business improvement methods. These tools are covered in the next chapter and can be used within or outside of the Six Sigma framework. It is important to note, however, that these tools will have maximum impact when used in unison with the prescribed Six Sigma framework.

Staff Implications

A top-to-bottom change within an organization does not happen overnight. Large organizations are often resistant to change, and poorly implemented programs have equally poor longevity. The Six Sigma doctrine prescribes an organizational hierarchy based on the participation and responsibility of each staff member within the program. The scope and complexity of this hierarchy sets Six Sigma apart from traditional quality improvement systems in the sense that the program is applied to the entire organizational chart instead of cordoning off a segment of statisticians to make recommendations for operations.

Instead of prescribing a method that relies on traditional silos, Six Sigma integrates the understanding of the DMAIC and the Six Sigma method into the organization at all levels. This "total organizational commitment" is also present in effective implementation of the Lean method, further evidence that radical change within an organization cannot be an effort composed of half measures.

The Six Sigma staff hierarchy divides each level of the organizational chart into colored "belts" or badges similar to the martial arts discipline judo. Each "belt" level has a specific and essential role in the success of the Six Sigma program's quality improvement measures and the success of Six Sigma's long-term integration with the organization's corporate culture.

fig. 6

Executive Leadership
- The top-level management responsible for establishing the Six Sigma vision (CEO, etc.).
- Enables the creation of the other Six Sigma implementation levels within the organization.

Champions
- Responsiblle for Six Sigma implementation across the enterprise.
- Act as trainers and coaches for Black Belt level staff members.

Master Black Belts
- Selected by Champion level staff.
- Ensure constant and consistent adherence to Six Sigma protocol, statistical measurements, and Six Sigma financial goals.

Black Belts
- Apply Six Sigma to specific projects.
- Devote all of their time to execution of process tasks in line with Six Sigma practices.

Green Belts
- Operating under supervision of Black Belts, Green Belts are rank and file employees.
- Have an understanding of Six Sigma in addition to their regular training.

White Belts
- Rank-and-file employees with limited-to-no training in Six Sigma practices.
- Normally do not participate in Six Sigma activities.

Organizational structures such as the belt hierarchy ensure that Six Sigma is uniformly applied and that each member of the organization knows his or her role. A notable characteristic of this staff organization is that some members of the enterprise dedicate their time to Six Sigma activities exclusively. This makes them unavailable for normal business duties, which is unattractive to many organizations.

Small organizations should also carefully weigh the pros and cons of adopting Six Sigma and must consider the demands that the program may place on their already limited labor pool.

To Recap

- The name of the Six Sigma program originates from the concept of standard deviation. Based on statistical analysis and the reduction of variation for significant quality improvements, Six Sigma is a comprehensive business improvement system that was designed first by tech conglomerate Motorola.

- Centered on the improvement process DMAIC and the design for quality process DMADV, Six Sigma offers structured approaches to process improvement and quality. DMAIC stands for Define, Measure, Analyze, Improve, and Control. These are not just a series of business activities that are finite, but rather a process that feeds back into itself at every step, creating a loop.

- DMAIC is a central thread that runs through the Six Sigma program and, by extension, Lean Six Sigma. Each sub process and statistical analysis task that is covered later in this text— and more complex, higher level ones that are outside the scope of this text—follow this same pattern and benefit from the DMAIC approach.

- To assign accountability and to provide a hierarchy to the organization, Six Sigma prescribes an organizational structure that reflects a colored belt system similar to martial arts disciplines.

Key Questions (answers on pg. 171)

1. Which of the following best describes the DMAIC process?

   a) a terminating series of steps that is performed just once

   b) a feedback-based improvement process that is performed continuously

   c) a supply chain theory management system

   d) DMAIC is not a process

2. The name "Six Sigma" comes from the Greek letter sigma which represents the arithmetical average of a data set (the mean).

   a) true

   b) false

3. The Six Sigma hierarchy uses a system of which of the following to denote rank and responsibility?

   a) colored cards

   b) alphanumeric call signs

   c) a progressive series of shapes

   d) colored belts

| 2 |

Six Sigma : Key Tools & Processes

In This Chapter

- The data-driven nature of Six Sigma is explored through the data collection process
- Not all data is created equal; different methods of collection and different kinds of data are defined
- Statistical analysis of data is covered in detail, and basic statistical functions are outlined
- Visual depictions of data (data plots) are explored

The Six Sigma approach is a process quality program that relies on statistical quantification, so it's no surprise that 6σ relies first on data. Once decision makers have defined their goals and gathered the relevant data, a wide range of statistical tools are available for use that interlock with select tools from the Lean toolkit.

Data Collection

Data collection, and its importance to the Six Sigma method, is a topic that comes up again and again. Six Sigma relies heavily on data and its collection, but the term "data" is so general and ambiguous that it could really mean just about anything. Understanding that there are different forms of data to be collected also leads decision makers to understand that different forms of data rely on different methods of collection.

Types of Data

Data can be broadly categorized as one of two categories outlined below.

Continuous Data

Continuous data is quantitative data measured on a continuum scale, and can be infinitely divided—this technical definition makes more sense when contrasted with the other types of data covered next. Continuous data represents activities such as call length, lead time, cost or price, and quantifiable characteristics like dimensions or temperature.

To use the last item as an example, if a part is forty inches long, it can be expressed as twice the length of a part that is twenty inches long, or it occupies the same length as four ten-inch parts laid end to end. In this example the unit of measurement—inches—is the continuum scale. The length can be infinitely divided or multiplied as we see fit. While there may be no need for four ten-inch parts laid end to end, we can conceptualize and express them mathematically. The same is true for call duration or lead time. Measured in units of time, the length of each falls somewhere on a number line representing the passage of time.

Discrete Data

Any type of data collected that is not continuous is discrete data. This is a general umbrella definition, and to narrow the focus, discrete data can be broken into the four subcategories shown below. Discrete data is so called because it *cannot* be measured on a continuous scale. It exists in discrete—or individual and terminating—quantities. Discrete data can be numerical or it can be categorical, another aspect that separates it distinctly from continuous data.

Numerical discrete data could be the number of parts in inventory or the number of defects recorded in each batch. Categorical discrete data could be the color of those parts or the answer to the question "Is this part red or blue?" The answer "It is blue" is categorical discrete data. In this way, discrete data can be both quantitative and qualitative.

- **Counts :** *Count data* is just as it sounds: the recorded count of a particular value. It could be the number of errors, the number of parts in production, or any value that represents a physical number.

- **Binary Data** : *Binary data* can only have one of two values. Binary data could be the answer to the question "Was the product delivered on time?" There is only one answer, and it is either yes or no. While there may be insights that can be gained from a yes or a no, such as a "no" answer signifying a defect, these interpretations don't change the nature of the raw data itself. Yes/no, true/false, and pass/fail are all common examples of binary data.

- **Attribute Nominal Data** : *Attribute nominal data* represents individual datum points that are labels. Attribute nominal data have no concrete relation to the objects or circumstances they represent, and therefore there is no value in attempting to analyze this type of discrete data. An example of attribute nominal data would be the assignment of numbers to departments (Dept. 1, Dept. 2, etc.). While it is important for the organization to be able to tell the departments apart, the labels themselves really have nothing else to tell us; in other words, they don't have a significant order or a measurable magnitude.

- **Attribute Ordinal Data** : In contrast to attribute nominal data, ***attribute ordinal data*** does relate to a real value. Attribute ordinal data are qualifying labels, such as an evaluation of performance: unacceptable, poor, acceptable, good, great. Each of those values represents a certain value, and therefore there is a significance to their order.

This characteristic is known as an ordinal scale, and while ordinal scales can be very helpful, they do not convey a degree of quantifiable difference between each value, nor do they convey magnitudes. The evaluation of performance example above is an ordinal scale consisting of five values, but there is no way to gauge exactly how different they are. The scale tells us that unacceptable performance is worse than poor performance, but there is (and cannot be) a degree to which that is the case.

fig. 7

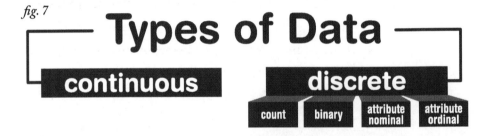

Input & Output

The relationship between data collected at various points within the process—whether it is production or a different business process—can be represented by the variables x and y. Generally speaking, business processes follow a standard pattern.

fig. 8

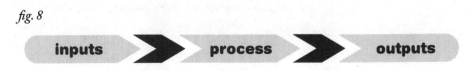

Predictor measures
=
Inputs/
Process

Inputs, such as customer requirements, materials, arrival times, and costs, are fed through the business process. The business process could be production, manufacturing, or it could be a service or function such as call center response time or billing activities.

Based on the inputs and the business process, outputs are generated. Both the inputs and process stages of the overall business process are considered "x factors," also known as ***predictor measures***. These leading indicators (lead measures) produce the business process outputs, otherwise known as "y factors." Also known as ***result measures***, y factors are lag measures that are dependent on the x factors that come before.

fig. 9

Customer satisfaction is a result measure (y factor). It is dependent on accuracy within the inputs, as well as a low defect rate within the process—both of which are x factors. Lead time is also an output or result measure. It is derived from the input of "arrival time"—when raw materials arrive—and the time required to complete all production processes.

A key component of the Six Sigma system is the monitoring and control of x factors—inputs and processes—to positively impact y factors—outputs. If problems with critical x factors can be identified, then they can serve as early warnings to problems that may arise with key y factors. Six Sigma's designers understood—as did the designers of Lean— that visibility leads to action. Defects that go undetected will not be rectified until they are part of the process output, and then it is often too late.

fig. 10

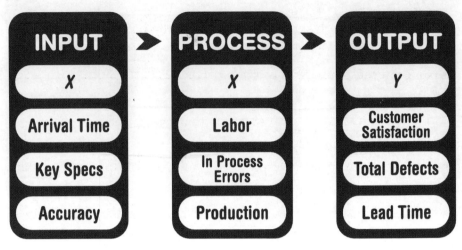

Data Collection Planning

Output data can be measured to generate a baseline or benchmark against which future performance can be measured. Inputs and process functions can be measured to determine sources of variation.

To produce actionable and useful information, however, data collection methods must do two things:

1. Measure the right things *(useful measurement)*
2. Measure things right *(statistical validity)*

In order to meet those two criteria, a data collection plan is created to target data collection efforts and to get the most out of the data collection process.

The following is a sample data collection planning chart. A data collection planning chart should be constructed for each process. It is important to remember that these charts are not set in stone. Decision makers can and should modify the data collection plan as needed to ensure that collection is efficient and helpful.

fig. 11

Data Collection Plan

Type	Metric[1]	Stratification Factors[2]	Operational Factors[3]	Sample Size[4]	Source & Location[5]	Collection Method[6]	Who Will Collect[7]
Input							
Process							
Output							
	How Will Data Be Used?[8]			**How Will Data Be Displayed?[9]**			

1. **Metric** : This is the selection of which metrics will be examined, or the target of data collection efforts. When selecting an appropriate metric, a preference for continuous data over discrete data will result in a greater overall evaluation utility. Thoughtful consideration must also be given to ensuring that the metric selected is representative of the overall performance of the process under evaluation.

    Metrics should be selected in a balanced way throughout a process to ensure the proper evaluation of several relevant *x* and *y* factors (lead and lag measures). Decision makers should use best judgment and brainstorming sessions to determine which metrics to use.

    While VOC information (the Voice of the Customer) *should* always be made available, during the creation of new processes it may not be. When VOC information is available, it can be used in conjunction with a *"measurement selection matrix"* to determine which *x* or *y* factors relate to specific customer requirements. The following sample measurement selection matrix has been constructed for the process of producing an ice cream cone and focuses on the y factor (output).

fig. 12

CUSTOMER REQUIREMENTS	OUTPUT MEASURES					
	Delivery w/in 2 mins	% of cones that match order on delivery	% of cones that match order before delivery	# of complaints about cone consistency	Temp on delivery less than 10°F	# of customer complaints about quality
On-Time Delivery	S	W	W	W	W	M
Right Ingredients		S	S	M		M
Cold	M		W	M	S	M
Attractive Presentation	W		W	M	W	M
	S = Strong		M = Moderate		W = Weak	

The customer requirements (also known as *critical-to-quality requirements*) are listed down the left side. Across the top are outputs. The correlation between an output measure and the corresponding CQRs is rated as strong, moderate, weak, or no relation. Those outputs (or inputs, or process attributes) that have strong correlation should be singled out as candidates for data collection activities.

Note : Because the pictured measurement selection matrix focuses only on y factors, the data collected are considered "lag measures." Data collected on x factors are considered "lead measures."

2. **Stratification Factors :** The identification of *stratification factors* is a critical aid in determining root causes later throughout processes. A stratifying factor—also known as a stratifier—is a factor that can be used to segregate data into subgroups. Once segregated into groups called strata, a problem that at the outset may have seemed complex can be tackled one factor at a time.

    Stratification creates a focus on the critical factors for a process, and this in turn greatly speeds up the investigation into root causes. The process of identifying stratifiers also provides decision makers with a deeper and more comprehensive understanding of the elements of each business process. The chart below is used to determine stratification factors.

fig. 13

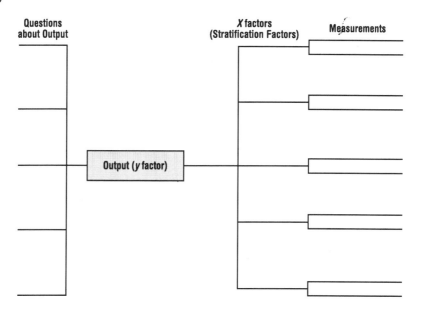

A *y* factor (output) goes in the center of the tree diagram. The chart stems out in either direction; on the left go questions regarding output. On the right, proposed stratification factors. These factors will be *x* factors (input and process variables). Stemming out farther right are measurements to define the *x* factors. The chart terminates with two binary decisions:

a. Does data exist to support these measurements?
b. Will these measurements help predict *y* (outputs)?

These questions will respectively determine the validity of the measurements and the predicting power of the x factors selected. When a process is being created, the stratifier identification process can be a trial and error brainstorming session. When applied to future processes, however, it will benefit from organizational learning and will become a better leveraged and streamlined process.

If the answer to question A is no, then the decision-making team should devise a method of measurement and data collection. Once data are available, even in a theoretical stage or simply as a sample, then decision makers can begin the process of determining the extent to which the data-type (x factor) can predict the y output in the center of the diagram. If the data-type proves to have little or no predictive power, then it is determined to be a non-critical stratification factor and other stratification factors should be evaluated.

3. **Operational Definition** : Operational definitions can be described as crystal clear instructions for the collection of data. These are agreed-upon and standardized methods of measurement. As with the Lean method, early designers of the Six Sigma system understood the value of the ***economies of repetition.*** That is to say that there's a direct correlation between the frequency with which an activity is completed and the accuracy of the end result.

The application of operational definition results in a consistent data collection methodology. This consistency, in turn, yields reliable interpretations. A decision maker's nightmare is attempting to sift through distorted data from inconsistent measurement methods.

Consider a customer service call center that tracks the average duration of incoming phone calls from customers. In order to secure consistent measurements of phone call duration, an agreed-upon initiation point for phone calls must be established. The initiation point may be the first ring; it may be the point at which the call is connected to an automated menu, or it may be the point at which the customer is connected to a live service representative. What's critical is that the initiation point is clearly established and consistently adhered to in all measurement activity. Operational definition is used to standardize data collection protocol and thereby ensure that the results obtained are not skewed.

4. **Sample Size** : The process of using a smaller sample to inform decisions about a batch or population as a whole is not unique to the Six Sigma method. Biologists, zoologists, meteorologists, and just about every other scientist who deals with statistical analysis uses sample sizes to infer attributes of a homogeneous whole from a portion of that population.

Sample size inference is a study in trade-offs. Data collectors can expect much shorter collection times when using a sample size method—they are only measuring a sample as opposed to all the data available—but no matter how advanced the sampling, there is always a level of uncertainty involved when not assessing the entire data set. The simple truth is that inferences made from a sample will never be quite as accurate as decisions made using the full data set.

The sheer size and scope of some true data sets would boggle the mind, however, and as such, sample size data collection still remains one of the most effective and intuitive data collection methods across homogeneous groups or populations.

Sampling can be broken into two categories: ***process sampling*** and ***population sampling***. This distinction is important because the tools for analyzing each type of data are different.

Traditional statistics applications focus on populations, whereas conventional business statistical applications focus on process sampling. The latter is preferred as it provides more insight into trends and contains a time-based component.

Population Sampling – samples drawn from a fixed group with definable boundaries. A parts inventory, a number of customer complaints, a batch of finished goods.

Process Sampling – samples drawn from a changing flow through a business that incorporates a time element. Due to the flowing nature of a process, it would be hugely inefficient to pull parts or units out of production to create a population for the ease of sampling. Instead, process sampling is best described as extrapolating characteristics of the process and the units flowing through it using systematic sampling (outlined below).

When it comes to statistically sound sample selection, it helps to know the two ways by which samples should not be collected: by *judgment* and by *convenience*. Either of these two methods will produce samples that are non-representative of the population or process.

The universally accepted best practices for obtaining samples are through random sampling and systematic sampling. Random sampling works best for population sampling. Systematic is the best fit for process sampling.

Systematic sampling can best be described as "sampling every nth unit." This could be as simple as sampling every third or tenth unit, or taking a sample every thirty minutes, but, broadly speaking, the larger the sample size obtained and the more economical the sampling process, the better.

5. **Source & Location** : Identifying the source and location of data boils down to whether the data is preexisting or needs to be generated for this application. The knee jerk reaction of decision makers is to use existing data, and if that is possible, then it is certainly a more cost-effective method of creating a benchmark, but decision makers should be aware of the following cautions for organizations that rely on preexisting data, aka "old data."

    The data must have existed under the same conditions. If the data is not recent and conditions have since changed, then the data is less likely to be useful. Therefore, when considering the use of preexisting data, the parity of current conditions vis-à-vis the conditions present at the time the data was collected must be verified.

    Going back to our customer service call center example—if we have preexisting data available measuring the duration of calls, where the call initiation point was defined as "the first ring," and we've since changed this initiation point to be defined as "the point of connection with a live service rep," then using our preexisting data to measure our current operational reality would become an apples and oranges comparison—a comparison between two things that have enough commonality to be in the same category but enough difference to make comparing them a futile effort.

    The data must have been collected in a transparent way. That is to say that decision makers should be able to authentically replicate the data collection process that was used to obtain the preexisting (old) data. This replication cannot be achieved unless the original data collection was conducted in a transparent manner. Transparency may also be aided via documentation of the original data collection methods. If the data was collected in a manner inconsistent with current organizational learning, or was collected in a way that invalidates it for use within the application at hand, then relying on such data would likely cause more harm than good.

There must be sufficient data to base conclusions on. Simply put, if there is insufficient data, then it should not be relied upon. Insufficient data fails to paint the whole picture, and making decisions based on insufficient preexisting data can produce "surprise" results in the future due to hidden or heretofore unknown data that was not included in the insufficient set. Preexisting or "old" data, when used properly, can supplement current data and establish historical trends. But as a best practice, old data should never be used as the sole means of assessing current operational realities.

6. **Collection Method** : The method of collection is specified. As with the Lean model, Six Sigma's designers understood that simpler is better, and for data collectors throughout the production process, the use of basic *checksheets* is recommended. Checksheets are easy-to-use straightforward data collection forms.

Each checksheet is tailored to a data collection task to ensure that not only is the data collected by different parties uniform, but also that critical stratifiers are included and not overlooked.

Checksheets are not set in stone. Their format and layout should often be revisited to assess effectiveness and relevance to the data collection task at hand.

Sample checksheets with corresponding notes can be found in the Appendix of this book.

7. **Who Will Collect** : Deciding where the responsibility of data collection falls, and ultimately to whom the data collection duties will be delegated, is an important task. Like a team of volleyball players all in pursuit of the same playable ball, the opportunity will only be seized if one player directly assumes responsibility; otherwise each player will hesitate, to avoid a collision.

The person who ultimately performs collection duties should be selected according to the following simple criteria:

Familiarity – Data collectors should be familiar with the process at hand.

Availability/Impact – Data collectors must have the required degree of availability to perform data collection activities with minimal impact on existing job duties.

Note : Keep the data collection activity short and sweet. Conventional wisdom holds that if you assign a person a data collection activity requiring more than fifteen extra minutes per day to perform, then it is not likely to be completed correctly on a regular basis.

Bias – Data collectors should be impartial. If the data collected has the potential to reflect poorly on the collector's job performance, then perhaps he or she should not be made responsible for that particular data collection duty.

There is no robust decision-making matrix or statistical method designed to aid in the selection of the right personnel for data collection; nevertheless, exercising good judgment, especially in consideration of the factors listed above, will produce superior results.

8. **How the Data Will Be Used** – Having a clear sense of how collected data will be utilized can help inform the collection process. Data collected for a root cause analysis, for example, will not be collected in the same way as data intended to determine baseline levels of product variation.

9. **How the Data Will Be Displayed** – This final section of the data collection plan identifies which statistical chart or method of display will be utilized. Example data displays include histograms, Pareto charts, scatter charts, etc. Data display charts are covered in more detail (and illustrated) later in this chapter.

Statistical Analysis

When discussing Six Sigma and Lean Six Sigma, it is impossible not to delve into the world of statistical analysis. While this text is in no way a comprehensive introduction to the world of statistics, certain methods of statistical analysis will be highlighted here for reference and instructional purposes.

The most useful data aggregates and displays are formed when a statistical analysis tool is chosen that best accommodates the data at hand. The inappropriate matching of a statistical analysis tool with data could result in, at best, wasted time and frustration, and at worst, incorrect inferences derived from poor or misleading presentations of data.

The field of statistics is generally divided into two categories.

Descriptive Statistics

Descriptive statistics refers to the analysis and/or graphical representation of data to describe a population. Identifying the mean (average) and median (midpoint) when describing data collected on the heights of teenagers in a geographic area would be an example of descriptive statistics.

Inferential Statistics

Inferential statistics involves the collection of small-batch sample data and using it to infer larger-scale conclusions or predictions about a population. When the cable company sends out an online survey—and let's say that on average only 2 percent of all customers fill it out—the cable company uses this limited representative sample of data (2 percent) to infer information about the widespread sentiment customers have about their cable service.

Measures of Central Tendency

Central tendency is best described as the tendency of data to cluster around average or "central" values such as the midpoint of the data. Thinking back to our normal distribution (bell curve) example from Chapter 1, normal distributions are heavily clustered around the center of the data, or the most common values.

The three most common *measures of central tendency* are the ones that just about everyone has heard of: mean, median, and mode.

Mean

The mean is the average of a set of data. This is specifically the arithmetic average of a set of data, meaning that it is calculated the same way every time using the standard mean calculation. This is the most commonly used measure of central tendency.

fig. 14

$$\overline{X} = \frac{\Sigma x}{n}$$

Where:

$\overline{x}$ = the mean of a sample (spoken or written out as "x bar")

Σx = the sum of all data values (capital sigma, the statistical summation operator)

n = the number of data items in the sample[1]

Median

The median is the midpoint of a ranked set of data. In this instance, "ranked" means that the data has been organized in ascending or descending order. Once this has been accomplished, the value in the middle of the range of ranked data is thē median. There will only be a "middle number" if there is an odd number of data points. If there is an even number, the median is instead the average of the two middle values. Median can be written as x (spoken or written out as "x tilde").

Mode

The mode is simply the most frequently occurring number in the set. This is most easily identified when the data range is ranked in either ascending or descending order.

To demonstrate these and future concepts, the following data set will be used.

---

[2] This equation is technically the equation for the mean of a sample. The alternative mean equation is for the mean of a population represented with the Greek letter μ or mu. The equation is the same, but instead of a lower case "n," a capital "N" is used to denote the number of data points in a whole population rather than a sample.

fig. 15

Collection of 30 Performance Scores*
*scores are out of 50 possible points

24	15	38
36	8	6
21	30	14
35	16	27
17	49	36
50	7	17
27	8	21
26	23	29
49	4	17
22	41	39

The mean of this set is 25.7. The numbers were added up and then divided by 30, the number of data points within the sample. To find the median and mode, the numbers must be ranked.

4, 6, 7, 8, 8, 14, 15, 16, 17, 17, 17, 21, 21, 22, 23, 24, 27, 27, 29, 30, 35, 36, 36, 38, 39, 41, 46, 49, 49, 50

The median is the middle number of the ranked data. Because there are thirty data points (an even number), the middle number is the average of the two numbers in the middle of the data set.

4, 6, 7, 8, 8, 14, 15, 16, 17, 17, 17, 21, 21, 22, | 23, 24, | 27, 27, 29, 30, 35, 36, 36, 38, 39, 41, 46, 49, 49, 50

$$23 + 24 / 2 = 23.5$$

The median in this instance is 23.5.

The mode is the most frequently occurring number, and in this data set the value 17 occurs three times, making it the mode.

Measures of Spread

Measures of spread, unlike measures of central tendency, concentrate on calculating variation within a data set. The simplest measure of spread is the calculation of range.

Range

Range reffers to the difference between the largest and smallest numbers in a set. Range is determined by subtracting the smallest number (the min) from the largest number (the max).

Referring back to our performance scores example, the min (smallest number) is 4, and the max (largest) is 50. Therefore, the range of scores is 46 (50 – 4).

Variance

Variance is a measure of the overall difference between the data values and the mean (average) for that set.

To determine the variation from the average, first the average must be calculated. From our example data set, we know that $\bar{x}$ = 25.7. Next, we calculate the difference between each data point and the average; in statistical terms this is expressed as $(x_i - \bar{x})$. Once those figures have been determined, each must be squared to ensure that the calculation proceeds using only positive numbers (variance is an absolute value-based measurement and cannot be negative).

Known as "the sum of the squares" in statistics, the next step is to total all of the squared values, then divide the result by $(n – 1)$ or the total number of data points less one. The resulting figure is expressed in units^2

or the square of whatever the original data's unit was ("performance scores squared" in our example). The full variance equation is shown below, followed by an example that matches our sample data set. In the world of statistics, the value for variance is represented by the variable *s*.

fig. 16

$$s^2 = \frac{sum\ of\ squares}{n-1} = \frac{\Sigma\,(x_i - \bar{x})^2}{n-1}$$

Note : This is the sum of squares equation for a sample. The sum of squares equation for a population has the "N" in the denominator instead of "n − 1."

For the sample data set, the variance is 188.2 performance points squared. If more of the evaluations had scored exceptionally higher or lower in our sample data set, then the variance would also be higher. If more of the scores were closer to the average, then the variance would be lower.

Variance is a measure that has advantages and disadvantages for decision makers. The key advantage is that variance is additive. This means that a process's total variance can be derived by simply adding together the variances from each step or data collection point.

fig. 17

Data Point	$x_i - \bar{x}$	Result^2
4	-21.7	472.34
6	-19.7	389.40
7	-18.7	350.94
8	-17.7	314.47
8	-17.7	314.47
...	...	...
41	15.3	233.07
46	20.3	410.74
49	23.3	541.34
49	23.3	541.34
50	24.3	588.87

Σ = 5457.87

Σ / n-1 = 188.20*

*The full chart can be found in the Appendix

The major disadvantage is that variation is expressed in units squared, which are difficult to correlate to the real world. Astute readers will ask, "Can't we just find the square root of the variance to reduce it to real units?" The answer is both yes and no.

Finding the square root of variance is the same formula for determining standard deviation, the statistical function at the heart of Six Sigma. While this calculation *does* produce actionable or real units of measurement by reducing the result of variation calculations to the standard units instead of units squared, standard deviation results are *not* additive.

If, however, a decision maker has determined the total variation for a process or system, *then* the square root can be taken to determine a total standard deviation. Simply adding the standard deviation values of aggregate subprocesses will not produce an accurate or true result.

> Standard Deviation – Standard Deviationis the average distance between each data point and the mean (arithmetical average). Standard deviation is represented by the Greek letter lowercase sigma: σ.

Standard deviation is much more helpful to decision makers due to the fact that it is expressed in the same units as the data collection (instead of units squared as variation (s) is expressed). Standard deviation is *not* additive, though, so the calculation for variation must be done first to determine a number from which the square root can be taken. In our performance scores example, we know that the variance is 188.2. The following is the formula for standard deviation. Note that it is the same formula as for variation (s) but with the added square root component.

Taking the square root of 188.2 produces a standard deviation of 13.7. This means that each data point is on average 13.7 units (in this case, performance points) away from the mean.

fig. 18

$$\sigma = \sqrt{\frac{\Sigma\,(X - \overline{X})^2}{n - 1}}$$

Plots

Decision makers need a way to make sense of the massive amounts of data they are trying to process at a given time, and the best way to do this is visually. Different statistical plots are best suited for different kinds of data, or to identify different trends. The following are some of the most common and useful plot types used by decision makers. Let's take a brief look at how they are constructed and applied.

Box Plots

Box plots, also known as "box-and-whisker diagrams," are an at-a-glance look at the variation of a set of data. Not only do box plots provide an instant picture of variation, but they can also be used to quickly compare multiple sets of data.

Box plots display data through their quartiles, or the three points that divide a set of ranked data into four equal portions (quarters).

Using the data from our sample data set, the quartiles are marked below as vertical lines—notice that there are *three* vertical lines used to delineate *four* segments of data.

fig. 19

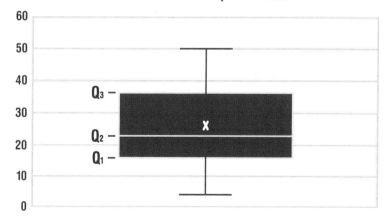

Box Plot of 30 Performance Scores Sample Data

fig. 20

4, 6, 7, 8, 8, 14, 15, │ 16, 17, 17, 17, 21, 21, 22, 23, │ 24, 27, 27, 29, 30, 35, 36, │ 36, 38, 39, 41, 46, 49, 49, 50

Becomes:

Q₁   **Q**₂   **Q**₃

4, 6, 7, 8, 8, 14, 15, │ 16, 17, 17, 17, 21, 21, 22, 23, │ 24, 27, 27, 29, 30, 35, 36, │ 36, 38, 39, 41, 46, 49, 49, 50

The main data display of the box plot is the shaded box at its center. The shaded box encompasses 50 percent of the data, everything between the first and third quartiles.

fig. 21

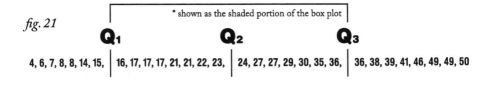

Box plots pack in as much info as possible about a data set. The band marked "Q_2" is the median of the data (the second quartile is always the median), and the x indicator marks the mean. The shaded box's range, from top to bottom, denotes the IQR, or ***interquartile range***. The IQR is the difference between the upper and lower quartiles. Marked with the letter Q, the quartiles are represented as Q_1, Q_2, and Q_3. Remember, the quartiles are the *values* that divide the data into four groups, not the groups themselves (that's why there are three, not four).

The IQR is determined by subtracting Q_1 from Q_3 ($Q_3 - Q_1$). Note that Q_2 is always the median. For our sample data $Q_1 = 15.5$, $Q_2 = 23.5$, and $Q_3 = 36$.

The graph's "whiskers" can denote a number of different data points. In our example above, the whiskers indicate the min (4) and max (50) of the performance scores. This represents the second 50 percent of the data; the first 50 percent is shown in the area of the shaded box.

fig. 22

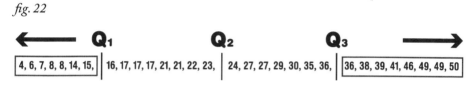

← Q_1 Q_2 Q_3 →

| 4, 6, 7, 8, 8, 14, 15, | 16, 17, 17, 17, 21, 21, 22, 23, | 24, 27, 27, 29, 30, 35, 36, | 36, 38, 39, 41, 46, 49, 49, 50 |

* the remaining 50% of the data is plotted inside the whiskers

Many decision makers use box plots to denote outlying, or extreme, data points. To qualify as outlying, data points must be ±1.5 times the IQR. In this instance a whisker would be drawn to the farthest point, and outliers in between would simply be plotted as data points. When a box plot is generated, the area between the whiskers represents 3 IQR or 1.5 times the IQR in the positive and negative direction.

Data points in the first and fourth quartiles—the data before Q_1 and after Q_3—will fall either inside or outside of these marks. To get the most accurate picture available, any data points that fall outside of the shaded box can be plotted individually with dots, but in most cases, only outliers that fall outside of the whiskers are plotted to draw attention to these extreme data points.

In many cases, outliers represent inaccurate measurements or errors in recording data, but this doesn't mean that outliers aren't worth investigating. If an investigation turns up evidence that the outliers represent real data, then the root cause of such a wild value should be investigated further.

Note : Box plots may be drawn vertically or horizontally.

Histograms

Histograms are also known as frequency plots. Expressed as bar graphs, histograms can be displayed horizontally or vertically. They are used for sets of continuous data and provide basic levels of insight.

An alternative to the traditional histogram is the dot plot, which is in essence a quick visual representation of the occurrence of each observation along a number line. Dot plots are best suited to smaller data sets (fifty data points or less), and they can be easily drawn by hand, making them an excellent choice for use "in the field."

fig. 23

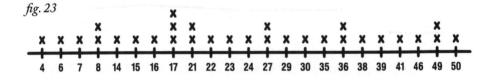

fig. 24

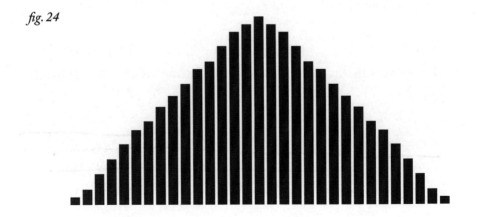

The previous histogram example (fig. 24) is a histogram that reflects normal distribution. This is representative of data that is more or less symmetrical about a central mean (arithmetical average).

Below is a histogram that exhibits what is known as bimodal tendencies, or a two-peaked distribution. This is reflective of a process that has two distinct pathways. In some cases, this will be a true representation or anticipated outcome of the data, but in many cases it will not. Investigation will be required to determine the cause of the divergent process path, and the DMAIC method of improvement should be applied to align the process with customer requirements.

fig. 25

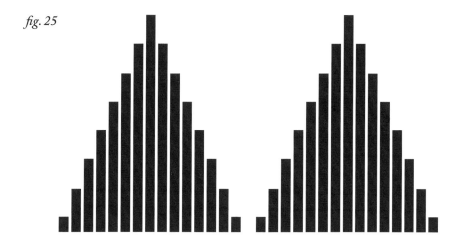

The following histogram exhibits a skewed distribution, or a histogram where the data is stacked on one side of the graph or another.

fig. 26

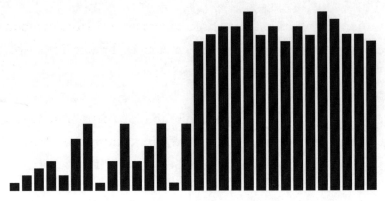

Scatter Plots

Scatter plots are key tools for visually representing and discovering trends within data sets. They demonstrate the correlation (relationship) between two factors or variables. When analyzing a scatter graph, the tighter the spread, the stronger the correlation. Scatter plots have a wide variety of uses, but most commonly they are used to demonstrate trends, develop or refine hypotheses, and can help predict the effects of some processes under other sets of circumstances.

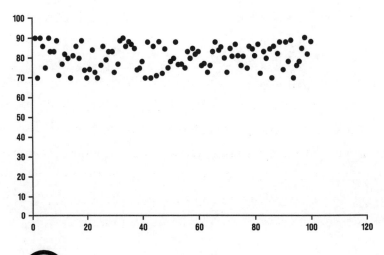

fig. 27: The pictured scatter plot has a high correlation; the spread is confined to between approximately 70 and 90 units on the y-axis.

To Recap

- Structured and proper data collection is a large component of proper implementation. Data can be broken into two broad categories: continuous and discrete.

- Continuous data is measured on a continuum scale and is infinitely dividable (characteristics like size, weight, and temperature).

- Discrete data is any other kind of data that is not continuous. This includes counted data (a discrete number of physical items), binary data (Y/N, pass/fail), attribute nominal data (data that consists of arbitrary labels), and attribute ordinal data (data that reflects an ordinal scale such as good, better, best).

- The basic business process consists of inputs moving through a process and generating outputs. These three stages can be expressed as variables or factors. Inputs and the business process itself are considered x factors, and the process output is termed a y factor. X factors can also be known as predictor measures or lead indicators, and y factors as result measures or lag measures.

- A thorough and structured data collection plan is necessary to guide decision makers to collect the right data accurately. Aspects such as the metrics to be collected, stratification factors, operational definitions, sample size and sampling procedure, source and location of data, collection method through the use of checksheets, appointing a data collector, intent of data, and method of data display are all outlined for decision makers.

- The mean represents the average, specifically the arithmetical average of a data set.

- The median is the middle value within the data set.

- The mode is the most frequently occurring data point.

- When calculating measures of spread such as range, variation, and standard deviation, the focus is instead on how far apart data points are. The range is the scope of the data, and it is derived from subtracting the smallest number (min) from the largest (max).

- Variation is the *additive* distance from the mean, though it is expressed in non-relatable units. Standard deviation is the *non-additive* distance from the mean for each data point, and it is expressed in units that are relatable and useful.

- Histograms are traditional bar charts, and these frequency diagrams are used to analyze the distribution of data quickly and easily. An "in-the-field alternative" to traditional histograms are dot plots, or plots for small sets (fifty data points or less) that use dots to represent the frequency of observation of specific values.

- Scatter plots demonstrate the relationship (otherwise known as the correlation) between two factors or variables. A tighter clustering of data points represents a stronger correlation, and a looser cluster a weaker correlation. A tight cluster representing a strong correlation does *not* guarantee a cause-and-effect relationship between the two variables.

Key Questions (answers on pg. 171)

1. Discrete data is data that can be measured on a continuum scale and can be infinitely divided.

   a) true   b) false

2. Binary data is best described as which of the following?

   a) pass/fail   b) true/false
   c) yes/no   d) all of the above

3. Which of the following best describes the Six Sigma interpretation of a business process?

   a) x factors such as output generate y factors such as input and processes

   b) x factors such as input and processes generate the y factor output

   c) the y factor output generates the x factors input and processes

   d) x factors do not impact the business process, only y factors do

4. Which of the following best describes a data collection plan?

   a) it is not important because data is always available

   b) it is very important to ensure consistent and accurate results

   c) it is not important because collection measures are at the discretion of production staff

   d) it is important because planning leads to goal accomplishment

LEAN SIX SIGMA QUICKSTART GUIDE

5. Which of the following are considered statistically sound sampling methods?

   a) judgment & convenience   b) pace & precision

   c) random & convenient   d) random & systematic

6. Standard deviation (σ) is helpful for which of the following reasons?

   a) it is a measure of central tendency   b) it is a measure of variation

   c) it is expressed in real units   d) it is expressed in the form "units²"

| 3 |

An Introduction to Lean Production

In This Chapter
- The Lean method of production is introduced and explored
- The various sources of waste are defined
- The guiding core principles of Lean are outlined

The Lean model for production and manufacturing is a collection of business practices, strategies, and methods that focus on waste elimination and continuous improvement within an organization. Often referred to simply as "Lean," this business model also applies to a wide range of industries, not just the manufacturing sector.

Lean's management philosophy was interpreted from the Toyota Production System. At the center of this business concept is the effort to eliminate three types of manufacturing waste: *muda*, *mura*, and *muri*. From the central doctrines of the Lean and Six Sigma programs, we can see a basic compatibility and a shared goal: the elimination of variation and the achievement of the highest possible levels of quality.

Muda represents waste, and it directly translates from Japanese as "futility" or "uselessness." Lean's main objective is to clearly separate the value-added activities from the activities that are identified as wasteful or non-value-added.

Mura is the concept of waste in the sense of unevenness. Unevenness in workflow means unnecessary downtimes or periods of unnecessary stress on equipment, systems, and workforce. Unevenness results in uncertainty, which leads to variation. Irregular or uncertain intervals are difficult to predict, and therefore forecasting becomes difficult. A high degree of uncertainty can also greatly reduce the responsiveness and effectiveness of an organization's supply chain.

Muri is waste created through overburden or through a failure to understand capabilities. This is a tangible concept when applied to facility layout and assembly and manufacturing processes; an overly burdensome workload can cause failure or increase rates of defective production. Overburden in conjunction with unevenness can also create expensive bottlenecking within an organization.

In tandem with the overriding value of waste reduction lies the philosophy of kaizen, or the creation of a culture of continuous improvement. This is a broad concept, and in practice it can be implemented in a multitude of ways that span diverse industries. Most of all, the real power of Lean lies in the creation of a vigilant mindset among the entire workforce, from workers on the assembly line all the way up to the CEO's office. This mindset reflects the unceasing efforts to reduce waste within processes and continuously improve the organization through innovations, both small and large.

Muda is the easiest of the three manufacturing variations to categorize. Almost all of the physical sources of waste within production processes fall into the classification of one of the following sources of muda. These sources can be summarized with the acronym *D.O.W.N.T.I.M.E* (see fig. 28).

Defective Production

Defective production is an obvious culprit of waste. Defects can incur cost through tangible outcomes such as scrap, retooling, repurposing, or reworking. Intangible costs include decreased brand perception and loss of market share. The elimination of defects is one of the core values that link the Lean and Six Sigma programs.

fig. 28

D	**Defective Production** Defects incur unnecessary costs, both tangible and intangible.
O	**Overprocessing** There is no need to further apply processes to a part that meets the customer's specs.
W	**Waiting** Waiting is a non-value-added activity. No matter how long a part has been "waiting," that time cannot be billed to the customer
N	**Non-Used Employee Talent** Underutilized employee talent represents cost and waste for the organization.
T	**Transportation** Defects incur unnecessary costs, both tangible and intangible.
I	**Inventory** Maintaining an on-hand inventory incurs costs and waste in other areas.
M	**Motion** Unneeded motion, in the form of processing or movement of parts, creates waste events.
E	**Excessive Production** Production that outpaces demand creates costs and waste.

Overprocessing

Overprocessing is a non-value-added activity, and therefore wasteful. Overprocessing waste events are the result of poor communication, ineffective or inefficient production controls, or other errors that cause a part to be processed past the customer's specs. Lean methodology dictates that any production past what is absolutely necessary is a waste event.

Waiting

Waiting is a status assigned to any time that a part is not being actively processed. Time spent waiting is non-value-added and therefore considered a waste event. Waste through waiting is tied to many aspects of production including evenness of workflow, facility layout, and process management.

Under-utilized Employee Talent

Under-utilized talent is a difficult source of waste to identify and harder still to quantify. The cost associated with this type of waste is best described as an opportunity cost, since the exact nature of the "price" is nearly impossible to calculate. This classification of waste is more in line with the kaizen ideology of continuous improvement, because it is addressed through training, communication, and team building exercises rather than statistical models and flow charts. It is a reminder to both management and rank-and-file staff members that innovation can come from all levels of an organization and that continuous improvement includes people, not just processes.

Transportation

Transportation that is not value-added is considered waste. This doesn't only include transportation from one facility to another or orientation within a warehouse but also encompasses movement from one workstation to the next and non-process-oriented movement on the factory floor. Transportation itself incurs cost, but the process of moving product exposes that product to possible loss and damage.

Inventory

Inventories of all types incur costs. Whether they consist of raw materials, work in progress, or finished goods, large inventories can contribute significantly to an operation's expense profile. Lean practitioners often use Just-In-Time (JIT) inventory control measures coupled with stable and even work flows to reduce on-hand inventory. We will examine JIT inventory in Chapter 4.

Motion

Motion causes a number of repetition-based costs. Wear and tear on facilities, machines, and other assets is the result of production cycles and other motion. Repetitive strain injuries, or the equivalent of wear and tear on a workforce, are also caused through motions in a process. While wear and tear is inevitable, unnecessary motion can reduce efficiency, cause bottlenecks, and shorten the lives of production machines.

Excessive Production

Excessive production as a source of waste events goes hand-in-hand with wastes relating to on-hand inventory. Excessive production increases the chances of defective production or can cause defects to go undetected within the quality control system. Additionally, the excessive finished goods must be stored or liquidated, both options resulting in financial costs. Lean prescribes small production batches and a method known as the "pull production system" to combat excessive production. The pull production system is described in detail later in this text.

Principles of Lean Production

The Lean production method uses a core doctrine of six guiding principles to outline the ways an organization can produce an environment and a culture centered on waste reduction, efficient business methods, and continuous improvement.

fig. 29

1. Continual Elimination of Waste

- Identify the eight sources of waste (DOWNTIME)
- Differentiate between value-added and non-value-added activities

2. Goals with a Broad View

- Goals drive tasks
- Tasks are matched with organizational objectives at all levels

3. Simplicity

- Simpler solutions are better solutions
- Complex problems can be broken down into simpler, smaller problems

4. Continuous Improvement

- Learning from the past is growth
- Understand how all six philosophies are related and interdependent
- Understand that what you build today is the foundation for tomorrow

5. Organizational Visibility

- Visible problems are solvable; invisible problems are not
- Visibility at all levels encourages continuous improvement

6. Flexibility

- The organization must be ready to respond to a changing market environment
- The organization must be ready to respond to changing customer needs
- The organization must be prepared to restructure to survive

The Continual Elimination of Waste

The first component of the Lean philosophy is addressed in the identification of muda and non-value-added activities. An organization that commits to reducing waste must also commit to seeking it out. There are many tools that exist for this purpose, several of which, such as value stream mapping and process analysis, will be discussed in depth in Chapter 4.

Goals with a Broad View

The second component of Lean philosophy deals with strategy and planning. Lean focuses on thinking strategically and incorporating long-term planning into everyday operations. In this way, the success and longevity of an organization should be compared to the overall industry in the long term, not matched to short-term gains. This methodology is not intended to trivialize short-term development but to put it in perspective toward maintaining a competitive advantage. Conceptually this can be implemented at the day-to-day level by matching tactical and operational tasks and decisions with strategic goals and avoiding a "tunnel vision" style of production. Tunnel vision production focuses on the product or the process and not on the customer, therefore making non-value-added activities harder to detect. In many cases this can lead to excessive production or production that does not consider the Voice of the Customer.

Simplicity

Simplicity is a golden rule in many fields. If companies "reap what they sow," then *simple in* means *simple out*, and a process that produces simple is simple throughout—so to speak. In other words, if simplicity is factored into each element of a process, then that process becomes simpler overall. Simplicity reduces the human error component in many cases and can mean that rectifying errors is easier as well. Simplicity also speaks to the Lean business model's waste reduction approach. Reducing a complex scenario into simpler parts alleviates energy wasted on complicated problems, and simple problems generally have simple solutions.

Simple processes are easier to teach and easier to implement. Simple configurations have lower chances of producing defects or errors due to malfunction or "moving part syndrome," in which defects increase with the number of moving parts. Simple operations are easier to monitor, and sources of waste are more easily identified. In some production applications, a simple approach may mean reducing the number of processes or cycles at a specific workstation. This may create more workstations, but it will improve flexibility and allow the process at each workstation to compensate for changing production needs or to address defective production.

Continuous Improvement

The kaizen culture built around continuous improvement affects an organization in the most positive way possible, because perpetual enhancement builds innovation on a foundation of existing success. Kaizen embraces all manner of innovation and revolves around the concept that frequent incremental changes produce stable and lasting results. A commitment to kaizen turns employees into engines for innovation that produce input at all levels. It is no secret that sweeping and rapid reforms can be hard to produce and difficult to repeat, but a company that adheres to continuous improvement will have already taken steps to producing an environment that is receptive to change, a characteristic that is an asset to any large organization.

In the original Toyota Production System, innovation arose from time spent dedicated to kaizen activities. These activities involved brainstorming, process observation, and mandatory improvement suggestions from all levels of staff. When specific issues arise and rapid innovation is necessary, a "kaizen blitz" approach is used. A kaizen blitz is an intensive improvement event including workshops, training, and guided discussion concerning the issues at hand.

Continuous improvement is not a onetime activity but the product of ongoing efforts. This cycle of process examination is referred to as the Plan–Do–Check–Adjust cycle (PDCA). This program represents the cyclic nature of activities that strive for continuous improvement. Kaizen activity can be represented as a series of steps that work in conjunction with the PDCA method.

- Set operations and activities to a uniform standard.
- Measure operations and activities to establish a benchmark.
- Compare benchmarks to requirements or goals.
- Increase productivity and reduce waste though innovation.
- Re-measure to establish a new benchmark and verify successful progress.
- Restart the cycle with the newly standardized operations.

Note : The PDCA cycle is also known as the Deming cycle or the Shewhart cycle. It is a business-oriented adaptation of the Scientific Method developed by the father of modern empiricism, Francis Bacon (1561-1626).

The planning stage of the PDCA cycle establishes objectives and intended methods. The "do" portion of the program is the execution of the plan. Accurate data collection at this stage is necessary for the next two stages and to measure goal achievement throughout. "Check" compares the data collected from the previous step against the goals established in the initial planning stage. The final adjustment stage is the implementation of corrective action based on the findings that have been gathered.

fig. 30

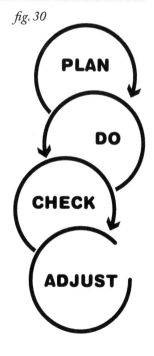

Visibility

The fifth element of the Lean philosophy is visibility. Visibility within an organization and within an organization's supply chain is much more than organizational transparency. Waste can only be eliminated if it can be identified, and invisible waste will go on unchecked indefinitely. This philosophy permeates all levels of operation, from the CEO's desk all the way down to the mailroom. In a practical, operational implementation, facilities should be open and uncluttered. Software systems should likewise be clean and uncluttered. Company correspondence and communication channels should never be chaotic or garbled. An organization with high visibility also has the distinct advantage of identifying issues before they arise. In situations in which staying the course means hitting an iceberg, an early warning can mean successful navigation to safer waters.

Visibility doesn't end with the organization. Depending on the strength and cohesion of supplier/buyer relationships throughout the supply chain, visibility can and should extend both upstream and down. High levels of visibility make forecasting easier and more accurate. Better visibility also results in a higher on-time rate for the entire supply chain network, as well as increased responsiveness. Additionally, Just-In-Time inventory methods, which we'll discuss in Chapter 4, are difficult to implement with poor supply chain visibility.

Flexibility

Flexibility is the final core component of Lean philosophy and an essential characteristic in the business world. Modern firms are no strangers to rapidly changing market conditions. Flexibility and continuous improvement go hand-in-hand in efforts toward making employees, as well as overall corporate culture, tolerant of and even hungry for change. A company that is ready to change is more prepared to succeed in the current business climate and will be more receptive to potentially innovative ideas. A focus on flexibility also means less friction in regard to changing customer needs. Resistance to the needs of the customer can result in intangibly damaging waste events in the areas of reputation or service perception.

To Recap

- The Lean production system is an interpretation of Japanese automobile manufacturer Toyota's revolutionary production system.

- Lean identifies and strives to reduce waste, expressed as muda (physical waste), mura (unevenness), and muri (overburden). Lean also prescribes a culture of continuous improvement known as kaizen.

- Different sources of muda can be identified by the acronym D.O.W.N.T.I.M.E., or defective production, overprocessing, waiting, non-used (or under-utilized) employee talent, transportation, inventory, motion, and excessive production.

- The Lean production system is centered on a guiding doctrine of six principles: the continual elimination of waste; maintaining goals with a broad view; engineering simplicity into processes and operations; the rigorous practice of kaizen (continuous improvement); organizational transparency and visibility; and flexibility or a willingness to accept change within an organization.

Key Questions (answers on pg. 171)

1. The Lean production system identifies three overarching sources of waste designated muda, muri, and mura. What do these three concepts represent?

   a) motion, transportation, and defective production

   c) waste, unevenness, and overburden

   b) waste, cost, and futility

   d) training, correction, and utilization

2. Which of the following is a D.O.W.N.T.I.M.E. source of waste?

   a) motion

   b) transport

   c) overprocessing

   d) all of the above

3. Kaizen is a core principle of the Lean production system. How does kaizen impact an organization?

   a) kaizen is a system of manufacturing best practices

   b) kaizen is a system of continuous improvement

   c) kaizen is a line change solution

   d) kaizen is a method of tool selection

| 4 |

Lean : Key Tools & Processes

In This Chapter

- The nuts and bolts of the Lean production method are explored
- The pull production system, a critical component of Lean success, is defined
- Process mapping and other visual communication tools are covered.
- The 5S workplace organization method is detailed
- Various components of waste reduction and efficiency improvement, such as Total Productive Maintenance and Rapid Setup methods, are defined

As an extensive waste reduction and production improvement system, the Lean method has an array of tools that can be drawn upon by decision makers to enhance the business operations of their organizations. Like Six Sigma, Lean is a program that requires total organizational commitment if results are to match expectations, and many of Lean's tools and processes reflect this aspect.

The Pull Production System

The *pull production system* is a central component of the Lean production model. It is a far cry from traditional production methods, which normally rely on forecasted demand and large batch sizes to leverage the cost savings associated with the economies of scale. While the specific forecasting methods may vary, the end result of traditional production methods is the same: demand is forecasted, raw materials for production are ordered based on those projections, and those materials are fed through the production process to produce finished goods.

This method is known as "*push production*" because the forecasted demand "pushes" the materials through production into finished goods. Organizations using the push production system will often produce surplus goods as a buffer against shipping delays or demand fluctuations. Push production relies on the economies of scale to reduce costs, and as a result the larger the production batch, the more cost effective the manufacturing process becomes.

Leveraging the *economies of scale* is the act of spreading out fixed costs over more units. If a part costs five dollars to produce at a rate of 10,000 units per week, with three dollars of that five dedicated to fixed costs and two dollars dedicated to variable costs, then economies of scale tell decision makers to simply make more parts to reduce the three-dollar (fixed cost) portion of the equation.

Variable costs are often tied to the volume of production. They include aspects such as the cost of raw materials—more units mean more materials consumed. Because units are mass-produced via a uniform process, the amount of material consumed for the production of each unit should be the same. Similarly, other intermittent costs such as labor, the rate of degradation to equipment, and consumables are also tied to the volume of production.

Whereas fixed costs are often tied to long-lived assets, variable costs (those that accountants refer to as PPE: property, plant, and equipment) include equipment wear and tear and utility expenses that *do not* vary with production volume. The rent on a structure, for example, does not change whether forty units or forty thousand units are produced in a week.

Line changes represent disruptions to production and downtimes that do not generate any revenue, but do generate cost, and with traditional push methods, line changes can be time-consuming. When time is money, even seconds become intolerable costs, so maximizing the number of units produced between line changes can mitigate costs.

By ramping up the number of units produced—otherwise known as increasing batch size—between line changes, that three dollars' worth of fixed costs from our example above could be squeezed down to one dollar per unit, if the rate of production was tripled. Tripling the batch size does not necessarily increase the costs of property, plant, and equipment (PPE), and those fixed costs are spread out over more revenue-producing units.

While fixed per-unit costs go down as the quantity produced increases, variable costs will go up—remember, these are costs tied to the volume of production. Calculating the rate at which variable costs increase depends on many case-specific factors. Experienced production managers scale production so that their increase in variable costs does not offset the savings gained through leveraging the economies of scale and reducing fixed costs.

The large-batch production characteristic of push production creates savings in one area while incurring potentially massive costs in another. In many cases savings are severely diminished by the costs of carrying additional inventory further down the supply chain. Ignoring these downstream costs is clearly oppositional to Lean's focus on identifying and reducing muda *through nearly every aspect* of D.O.W.N.T.I.M.E. sources of waste. The push production model, through reliance on artificial demand, also fails to adequately heed the Voice of the Customer.

The pull production system, on the other hand, turns each one of the shortcomings associated with traditional push systems into value-creating strengths. Instead of anticipated or artificial demand, the pull production system relies on *actual* customer demand. Instead of generating the demand via forecasting, then using that demand to push materials through production, the pull production system responds to actual customer demand in real time, using this demand to generate orders for raw materials, which are then *pulled* through the production process to accommodate immediate, clear, and present demand.

fig. 31

The Pull Production System

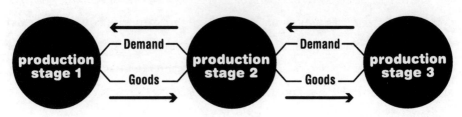

But what about line changes and the economies of scale? How can the pull production system only make enough of what a customer needs, then move on to something else and still do it profitably?

For the transition to the pull production system, everything had to change. Small changes to the push model would create greater waste events; the pull production system is a completely different and customer-centric approach to the manufacturing process.

In order to effect a massive increase in flexibility and responsiveness, the costs associated with line changes must be reduced, so faster changeovers and rapid setups can be innovated and perfected. The result is the ability to produce a variety of batch sizes to fit customer demand and the advantage of being able to quickly execute line changeovers.

To reduce the amount of buffer time and safety stock, a speedy and precise inventory and production method known as Just-In-Time ensures that the right amount of goods arrive in the right place at the right time. We'll discuss Just-In-Time, along with several other Lean implementation tools, in the following sections of this chapter.

Additionally, the flexibility and responsiveness of the pull production system rely on the interconnected nature of Lean. Each measure of waste reduction and innovation through kaizen supports and enables the flexibility and strength of the pull production system.

Process Mapping

The visual documentation of a process is an effective tool for defining the characteristics and aspects of that process. A type of visual documentation known as ***process mapping*** can serve as an investigative tool to find the sources of problems using easy-to-digest data. Process maps are also effective process communication tools for entities both within and outside of the organization.

A process map consists of a start-to-finish visual representation of a process; it can be a production process or any business process. The following example is a high level view of the process "Delivery of an Ice Cream Cone."

fig. 32

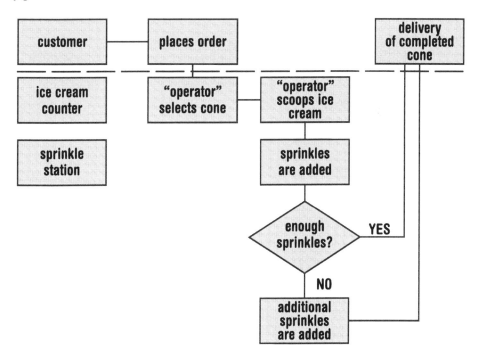

When creating a process map there are several key points to remember:

- **No matter how comprehensive, documentation is always subordinate to observation.** Seeing the process firsthand, and gathering useful insight and observation, is always more accurate and productive than relying on documentation.

- **A flowchart is a tool.** The inherent value of a process map or flowcharting tool is just as a tool. Mapping every process simply for the sake of mapping is not value-added activity, and it is not productive. When mapping a process, do so with a goal in mind, and have a role for the finished map as a tool in a larger business improvement sense.

  To this same end, process maps are meant to be used, not left in a drawer or in a folder on a computer server. Take the time to construct them correctly and use them later to produce real, actionable results.

- **Involve multiple people.** A process map that relies on the input of a single person is not a sound endeavor, and it may contain bias (consciously or unconsciously).

Process maps and flowcharts can be broken into two categories based on their level of detail.

High Level View – This shows the major elements of a process and the ways in which they interact with one another. This comprehensive map favors a bird's eye view over detail, which makes it better suited to establishing the scope of a project at its outset, but not ideal for process improvement down the line—there is often insufficient detail for high level view processes to be instructive.

Low Level View – This is mapping or flowcharting at the ground level, best suited for specific actions or detailed looks at specific elements of a process. It's not helpful for an overview of a process or system.

When using process maps, flowcharts, and value stream maps (next section) understanding exactly how they can be helpful informs how they will be constructed and which level of detail will be most useful. Process maps can be used to describe a process either "as is" or in its ideal (future) state.

As Is – As is process maps are records of the process in its current state. These can be used as reference tools, communication tools, or can serve as benchmarks against which future innovations can be compared.

Ideal – Ideal state process maps are sketches of the ways in which a process *could* work if certain changes were implemented. These maps serve as helpful "what if" scenarios in an effort to determine the potential waste elimination and efficiency gains that could be had if innovations or—in the case of high-waste processes—corrective measures were to be applied.

When creating a process map keep the following tips in mind.

- Stick to the agreed-upon level of detail
- Maintain a clearly defined process flow that is both easy to follow and continues in the same direction throughout the map
- Always follow up the creation of a process map with a discussion of the results. Do the results match production realities? Is the process map an accurate representation of the same process that it details?
- Due to the rate of innovation it is extremely important to date and title a process map. Decision makers should be able to understand what they're looking at in a glance

SIPOC

Differing from a traditional process map, a ***SIPOC diagram*** is a project-critical snapshot that conveys crucial information regarding a project, system, or process. SIPOC stands for Suppliers, Inputs, Process, Outputs, and Customers.

SIPOC diagrams help decision makers identify project boundaries and scope, as well as to identify a high level view of a project's flow from upstream to down. The high level view of SIPOC diagrams also helps decision makers quickly categorize multiple processes as having the same suppliers, inputs, process steps, outputs, or customers. For SIPOC diagrams to be optimally effective, they should include a minimal number of steps under each heading.

The example SIPOC diagram covers the process of producing ice cream cones (fig. 33).

fig. 33

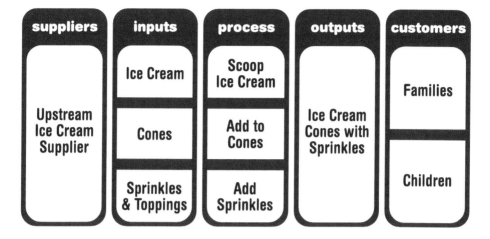

Spaghetti Plot

Spaghetti plots are versatile visual representations of data in the context of flow through a system. They are a clear companion to the Lean method with its focus on flow and evenness of production. The name comes from the long and wavy data depictions; the trends resemble long noodles laid out. When applied in a business environment, these visual charts are often referred to as *workflow diagrams*."

With statistical applications across all fields of science, from biology and zoology to meteorology and climatology, even the fields of medicine and pharmacology implement spaghetti plots to track flows. When the concept is applied to business, it can become a valuable tool that demonstrates exactly where waste events occur, not only in process flow, but in inefficient transport, motion, and facility layout.

As with so many of the tools in the Lean toolkit, the goal of implementing spaghetti plots is to identify waste through the clear differentiation of value-added and non-value-added activity. When used to track a product through each production workstation, or for the layout of an office, workshop, or storage area, the overlaying lines can be instructive to decision makers in regard to where streamlining should occur and how to address layouts to consolidate efforts.

To build a spaghetti plot of a workspace, follow these steps:

1. Map the workspace as it physically occurs.
2. Merge the steps of a process with the map by plotting each step in the appropriate location on the map.
3. Connect the plotted points with arrows to indicate direction of flow.

The resulting chart is a visual display of the flow of work through the mapped space and can serve to inform layout and workflow decisions. Look for areas where lines cross one another frequently. These areas should be addressed and redesigned for a cleaner flow and to eliminate the additional labor of backtracking. If there is a single station that sees paths coming back multiple times, the work that is completed there should be investigated to see if it can be done at the same time to save wasted labor and movement.

Value Stream Mapping

fig. 34

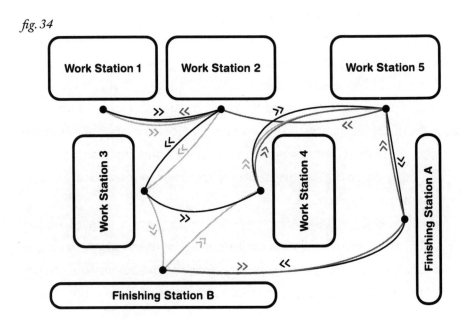

Value stream mapping is used to analyze the current state of all activities and processes of a product or service from absolute beginning all the way through to the end user (customer). This tool is also used to design new processes and methods and can be a valuable asset in identifying waste and differentiating it from strictly value-added activities. The goal of effective value stream mapping is to identify opportunities for improvement in the areas of cost, waste, and efficiency.

Value stream mapping is a complex process that requires a much more in-depth approach than standard process mapping or traditional flowcharting, but it is invaluable when it comes to the identification of waste in the areas of time and cost, and once waste is identified it can be eliminated. Visibility leads to action, and invisible problems cannot be solved—though their effects may be felt on operations.

Implementation requires identification of a particular product line, product family, or service. To get the most out of a value stream map, select one of the former that fits as many of the following criteria as possible.

Common Flow – There are similar steps within each of the subprocesses—in other words, don't compare apples and oranges.

High Volume & Cost – Value stream mapping efforts are complex and very time-consuming. They have their greatest effect when identifying waste in the form of cost and time, so a high-volume, high-cost process will benefit most.

Relevant or Critical Process – For relevant or critical processes, a value stream map is a worthwhile effort. Additionally, critical processes will have an impact on customer satisfaction, so they should be stripped of as much waste as possible.

Because a value stream map considers all of the inputs of a process, it is drawn in stages with each input flow added in overlay.

1. The first flow is the process flow. The construction of the map should mimic the way demand moves through production. This means starting with the customer and working backward (upstream). Constructing the process map includes identifying the main activities, then placing them in sequence on the map. This first stage is similar to standard process mapping activities.

2. Once the process flow has been added, the second set of inputs to map is the material flow. Material flows demonstrate the movement of all materials relevant to the process being mapped. Testing, data collection points, and all other activities related to QC (quality control) should also be marked within the material flow. The material flow is added in parallel and as an overlay to the process flow. Suppliers are added to the beginning of the map at the opposite end of customers.

3. Next, add information flows. These consist of elements such as parts orders, scheduling, tracking, and interaction between different elements (such as process and supplier, or process and customer). In this instance, the information flows are representing communication points—communication between the supplier and the organization's production, for example, or the methods by which the organization communicates with customers.

4. The value stream map is then updated with an overlay of process data. This data is best gathered right on the production floor and should conform to the following pattern of data gathered for each step.

- Trigger[1]
- Setup Time and Processing Time Per Unit
- Number of People (involved throughout the processes)
- Downtime Percentage[3]
- Takt Rate[2]
- Percent Defective Production (scrap rate)
- WIP Down Upstream[4]
- Cost of Links[5]
- Batch Size

[1] The trigger is the action or activity that starts the step.

[2] Takt rate is a calculation of the rate of production relative to customer demand. It can be expressed by the following formula.

fig. 35

$$T = \frac{T_a}{D}$$

Where:

T = Takt time (takt rate)

T_a = Work time per period (net available work expressed as time)

D = Customer demand or simply demand (expressed as production units)

Takt time is *not* a recording or calculation of the actual duration of unit production, but rather a metric that identifies production flow and prescribes production line parameters.

[3] Downtime percentage includes times when people, machines, or computers are not reaching full productivity because of some barrier.

[4] WIP is work in progress. The amount of work in progress at a given time in a process is an indicator of the overall volume utilization of the process. For example, if a process can accommodate 200 units of WIP to operate at 80 percent of capacity, and it is only carrying 140 units, then the process is instead operating at 56 percent capacity.

[5] Cost of links data records the cost of creating visibility and

communication between different elements of the process and other entities both within and outside of the organization.

5. Add process times and lead times to the chart. The addition of this data completes the chart and it is ready for review and verification. The value stream map should be verified with people who aren't members of the team but who are familiar with how the process works. If the value stream map can be confirmed with suppliers and customers, then it should be. Finally, review the value stream map for accuracy with those who are most familiar with its operation.

Value stream mapping represents one of the most complex and holistic tools available from the Lean toolbox for the identification and elimination of waste.

Value stream mapping involves seven primary methods of evaluating and analyzing processes within a value stream.

- Process Activity Mapping
- Supply Chain Responsiveness Matrix
- Production Variety Funnel
- Quality Filter Mapping
- Demand Amplification Mapping
- Decision Point Analysis
- Physical Structure Mapping

Further explanations of these methods and the Lean business model can be found in *Lean QuickStart Guide: The Simplified Beginners' Guide to Lean*, another title in the ClydeBank Media library.

5S

Respect for people and respect for the workplace are goals that are as lofty as they are nebulous. In order to ensure that these two important aspects of Lean implementation are sufficiently addressed, the *5S method* is prescribed as a clear way to measure expectations for both employees and management.

Often hailed as the guidelines that enabled the timeliness of JIT manufacturing, and the foundation of the powerful kaizen culture, the 5S method can come across as humble or underwhelming at first glance, but it is in fact a powerful workplace organization method. The 5S model derives its name from the five Japanese terms seiri, seiton, seiso, seiketsu, and shitsuke. Written in the Latin alphabet, each of the words starts with the letter 'S,' hence the name. The 5 S's translate loosely as sort, segregate, shine, standardize, and self-discipline.

fig. 36

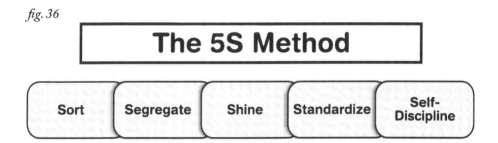

Sort

The *sort* portion of the 5S method can be quickly summarized by the phrase "everything has a place." Sorting is a practical extension of the Lean focus on waste reduction. When a workstation or an employee's work area is "sorted," everything is in its place. Unnecessary items, or items that are not needed at hand, are stored properly. If disposal is required, then these items are disposed of properly.

These simple concepts can expand to encompass a diverse range of circumstances, objects, and materials. A sorted workplace is one that defies the accumulation of unwanted or waste materials. This means that there are fewer obstacles to productive flow—a workstation that is free of debris is an efficient workstation—and that waste material is removed from the production stream. This macro-scale concept trickles down to the very micro scale of single employee workstations and even areas where employees may store personal effects, such as lockers and break areas.

Proper and thorough sorting does come with an administrative cost, however: it is necessary to constantly evaluate which items and materials are in fact necessary on the work floor and which should be stored or disposed of. These evaluation activities are often carried out by a dedicated supervisor or frontline level leader and can take time away from other value-added activities. Additionally, if items are deemed "unnecessary" but are not waste or are not in need of disposal, then they must be stored correctly. This consumes space, time for transport, and time for the coordination of storage.

Storage areas should be red-tagged as necessary to prevent the accidental reintroduction of unnecessary materials and items back into the production stream, or to reinforce the fact that they are only needed in some circumstances.

The rationale for these costs and additional work, of course, is that overall productivity is increased and workflow is undisturbed through obstacle-free production. Sorting strives to reduce waste events across the board but focuses particularly on reducing unevenness (*mura*) in workflow.

Segregate

The *segregate* aspect of the 5S method is the next logical step after sorting. While sorting identifies which items are necessary, segregation is the practice of organizing those items in such a way that they will produce the most efficient benefit. Segregation activities include arranging tools so that the highest-use tools are closest at hand. It means ensuring that the people who have a constant or consistent need for tools and materials can easily locate and access those tools or materials, and that all of their work can be done in the most efficient manner possible.

Just like every other aspect of Lean, segregation is not a onetime activity. Segregation activities should regularly be subjected to PDCA-style review, and those employees responsible for segregation activities should be empowered to make changes as the need arises.

Sorting and segregation are interrelated processes, as are segregation and the next "S," shine. In one interpretation of the 5S method, segregation and shine are combined into a single activity, effectively producing an alternative 4S method. This is reflective of the kaizen approach that makes up the backbone of Lean methodology: always be improving, always be learning, and always be flexible.

If, in implementation, it makes more sense to aggregate 5S methodologies into single, hybrid activities, then that is what should be done. Stretching an organization to fit the Lean model is a backward approach and a losing proposition. Instead, Lean— and the 5S method—should be stretched and tweaked to fit the organization and its unique production activities, culture, and specific production processes.

Shine

Shine embodies the concept that cleanliness is next to godliness (so to speak). It is sometimes referred to as "sweep" or "scrub." Not only do employees who work in a clean and well-maintained workplace have more respect for their employer and their responsibilities, but there are a number of practical benefits of a continuous commitment to cleanliness.

Regular cleaning of workstations and equipment means that there are no barriers to efficient production and labor. Just as the 5S practice of sorting eliminates unnecessary objects and materials to ensure an even workflow, a clean and orderly workstation is always ready and easy to navigate. Regular cleaning is a preventative measure as well; it reduces the effects of wear and tear on equipment and can prolong the life of critical production components.

A clean work environment is also the foundation of a safe work environment. From the very rudimentary practices of cleaning spills and clearing debris that can cause slips, trips, and falls to the more advanced activities that ensure that safety equipment can work without impediment, cleanliness is a vital component of safety.

Cleaning activities can serve another purpose: cleaning as inspection. Thorough cleaning already takes a deep dive into equipment and workstations—why retrace your steps a second time for a follow-up inspection? Scheduling cleaning routines to coincide with maintenance inspections saves time and effort. Cleaning routines can also be employed to maintain and monitor other 5S method activities such as sorting and segregation.

The effectiveness of a rigorous shine program is often evaluated using the following phrase: "Anyone not familiar with the environment should be able to detect problems within 5 seconds from within 50 feet." These "unfamiliar" people are often employees or supervisors from other areas who are tapped to perform visual inspections.

Standardize

Standardization is a common theme within the Lean framework. Standards provide benchmarks by which performance can be measured, and if performance can be measured, areas of opportunity for improvement can be identified (and improvement must be continuous). The standardize portion of 5S serves to ensure that all other 5S activities are targeted, productive, and goal-oriented.

Just as all the tools and equipment on the production line and at employee workstations must be in their places, so too must the 5S activities be organized and monitored. Standardization codifies best practices and maintains the organization's intent and standards in all aspects of deployment.

Self-Discipline

The **self-discipline** aspect of 5S is also known as "sustain" in some iterations of the 5S method, and it ties all of the other 5S activities together in a manner that is characteristic of the Lean framework. The definition, and therefore translation, of *shitsuke*, the fifth "S" in Japanese, is nuanced and complex. Sustaining and self-discipline are both only parts of the concept behind the word.

Shitsuke is associated with two definitions, and the complexity of the concept is somewhat diminished in translation. The first definition is more akin to discipline in the forceful sense of the word—it takes force to align all of the 5S methods into place. In this sense, the barriers of change are understood and described. Once these changes are in place, the second and more prevalent meaning of shitsuke becomes relevant. This is the process of self-discipline that is more in line with the English definition: the structured and conscious effort to maintain standards and practices. To do what is necessary "without being told."

The aim of this text is far from an exploration of Japanese language and culture, but the above example is instructive to students of the Lean philosophy in the idea that Lean is far more than simply a rulebook for productive and efficient manufacturing. Examples like the one above underscore the fact that Lean is a complete overhaul of an organization's culture and perspective, and it should be viewed as such.

A commitment to the letter of Lean while failing to commit to the spirit will only produce half-measures of success.

Eliminating Waste & Increasing Efficiency

True to Lean form, making things visible leads to action, and invisible problems can go on indefinitely. We know that kaizen is the culture of continuous improvement that is a common thread running through the entire Lean model, and that the vigilant elimination of waste in the forms of muda, muri, and mura are also key components of Lean operations, but in order to begin to innovate waste out of a process, that waste first has to be found.

To measure performance, decision makers use metrics from collected data that are compared to a benchmark—how it was versus how it is—and identify if efficiency has increased, stayed the same, or gone down. Metrics of time efficiency are powerful tools to this end.

Process Cycle Efficiency

Process cycle efficiency, or PCE, is one of the best, and simplest, measures of a process's efficiency and performance. PCE is a product of the measure "value-add time" or the time that is spent by the process to effect changes in materials to produce fitness for the customer's needs (also known as utility).

Value-Add Time – The total duration of all periods during a process when value is added through the creation of utility. It is calculated by finding the sum of all value-added time throughout the process.

fig. 37

$$\text{process cycle efficiency} = \frac{\textbf{value-add time}}{\textbf{process lead time}}$$

Process Lead Time – a value calculated through the application of Little's Law (next section). Process lead time is the time between the initiation and completion of the production process. PCE values are at-a-glance indicators of improvement, and they allow dissimilar processes to be compared to one another in terms of efficiency.

Little's Law

Little's Law is an equation used to describe process lead time, a component of PCE calculation. The equation is shown below.

Workstation Turnover Time

Workstation turnover time (WTT) is not related to PCE and Little's Law calculations, but it is still an important tool for decision makers and process designers when it comes to finding and tackling waste within a process.

fig. 38

$$\text{process lead time} = \frac{\textbf{number of things in process}}{\textbf{avergae completion rate}}$$

WTT is a measure of how long it takes a workstation to run a complete cycle of production on one "thing," such as a unit of WIP or a unit of finished goods.

fig. 39

$$WTT_k = \Sigma\,[(\text{setup time}_i) + (\text{process time}_i * \text{batch size}_i)]$$

Where

k = the process step (the specific activity within the process)

i = the number of things worked on in k

Total Productive Maintenance

Total productive maintenance (TPM) is the drastic reduction of unscheduled downtime from standard levels. These levels vary from industry to industry, but traditional push systems often cite the figure 30 percent in regard to downtime caused by equipment malfunction or failure. On the other hand, organizations that rely on the TPM method have reported reductions in mechanical failure and downtime to just 5 percent of all production time.

TPM relies on a number of common sense approaches to preventative maintenance and machine upkeep, while standardizing and prescribing a best practices method. TPM is beneficial to *all* organizations that rely heavily on high-cycle or heavy-use machinery, not just the production and manufacturing sector.

TPM, and the field of equipment maintenance in general, prescribe two types of mechanical maintenance.

Preventative Maintenance – Maintenance that occurs at regular intervals. Intervals could be based on time or utilization. For example, maintenance should be done every three months or 15,000 cycles, whichever comes first.

<u>Predictive Maintenance</u> – Maintenance performed based on indicators or diagnostic results that indicate machine deterioration. For example, a lubricant hose is damaged. We know that it will leak if not replaced and a lack of lubricant within the machine will cause damage and downtime, so the hose is replaced as an exercise of predictive maintenance.

To implement a TPM program, first the current state of all operating conditions must be established. This is done through the use of a form like the chart below.

	Availability	
A	Total Time Available	(mins)
B	Planned Downtime	(breaks, meetings, scheduled maintenance), (mins)
C	Run Time	(A-B), (mins)
D	Unplanned Downtime	$(D_1 + D_2 + D_3)$, (mins)
D_1	Breakdowns	(mins)
D_2	Changeovers	(mins)
D_3	Minor Stoppages	(mins)
E	Net Operating Time	(C-D), (mins)
F	Available Percentage	[(E/C) * 100%]
	Performance	
G	Processed Amount	(total units)
H	Design Lead Time	(ideal), (min/unit)
I	Performance Percentage	[(H*G)/E] * 100 (expressed as %)
	Quality	
J	Total Rejects	(units)
K	Quality Percentage	[(G-J/G)]*100 (expressed as %)
OEE	**(Overall Equipment Effectiveness)**	**(F*I*K) (expressed as %)**

fig. 40 : The value of OEE is the result of a number of preceding calculations. To help illuminate the progression of the OEE formula, each element is assigned a letter, and the component calculations of OEE are represented by formulas that employ these assigned letters for the sake of simplicity.

Once a benchmark, or the current state of processes, has been established, then standard TPM activities can be undertaken. TPM activities represent the standardization of common sense mechanical maintenance activities, and while all machines will be different from one another, there are some basic guidelines that should be followed to reduce unscheduled downtimes.

These steps are considered part of larger "solution phases" and should be carried out in a prescribed method that allows each step to build upon the last.

Solution Phase 1: **Return the Equipment to a Reliable Condition**

In order to effectively begin a maintenance regimen, the equipment in question must be returned to a reliable condition so that operators and technicians can start with a clean slate, so to speak.

This way, staff who will be servicing the equipment will know that any issues are not stemming from a history of poor maintenance. Resetting the condition of all equipment will also benefit service personnel when troubleshooting the source of future issues. Resetting equipment includes the following procedures:

- Cleaning thoroughly
- Addressing physical imperfections
- Changing consumables (filters, lube, etc.)
- Clearing debris
- Clearing away any unnecessary tools or supplies from the equipment area

Once the equipment is cleaned and serviced, it can be inspected for needed repairs beyond the scope of simple filter replacements and basic service. Color-coded tags should be used to identify areas in need of repair, and the issue should be recorded in a maintenance logbook. A standard TPM system uses the following color-significant tags to flag needed repairs:

- Orange for oil leaks
- Green for coolant leaks
- Yellow for air leaks
- Pink for machine defects
- Blue for electrical problems

Scheduling should be done to ensure that the equipment is available for needed repairs. It is the TPM project leader/team leader's responsibility to ensure that repairs are completed, but they should be completed by a qualified technician or repair specialist.

Solution Phase 2: **Eliminate Breakdowns**

In tandem with the equipment repair element of the prior solution phase, the reasons for repairs should also be examined to eliminate breakdowns of equipment. This often means doing the following:

- Securing fasteners, fittings, and bolts
- Replacing missing parts
- Replacing mismatched, worn, or incorrectly sized parts
- Cleaning and tracing the source of leaks, spills, and splatters

Issues similar to any of the above should be logged, and access should be made more conveniently available to problem areas so that regular maintenance can be completed quickly and easily.

Solution Phase 3: **Develop a TPM Database and Action Plan**

Solution phase 3 is often best completed by a team rather than a single planner or decision maker. A comprehensive list is developed that guides TPM activities related to what preventative maintenance must be completed, when (and how often) it needs to be completed, and by whom it is completed.

Solution Phase 4: **Eliminate Defects**

Building on the best practices outlined in the preceding solution phases, operators and technicians respond to issues via action plans. Adherence to the TPM program reduces defects and, ideally, operators and technicians are further trained to recognize warning signs of machine failure. This advanced development, coupled with thorough preventative maintenance practices, keeps production equipment running and reduces disruption to a bare minimum.

Rapid Setup (SMED)

If TPM can be considered keeping the trains running on time, rapid setup protocols (also known as "single minute exchange of die," or SMED) are the fast loading and unloading of those metaphorical trains.

With the reduction in batch sizes and increase in flexibility that the pull production method strives to provide, new issues are brought to the forefront. During mass production that utilizes large batches, the economies of scale are leveraged to spread the cost of inevitable line changeovers out over as many units as possible, and line changes are scheduled to be as minimally disruptive as possible. When the size of the batch production shrinks, the number of line changes that are necessary increases substantially, and in the kaizen spirit of reducing both downtime and D.O.W.N.T.I.M.E. waste, methods of efficient changeover follow the decision to switch to small batch production.

"Single minute" does not literally mean that all line changes should have a duration of only one minute; rather it means that they should not exceed ten minutes (single digit minute duration). While there is no prescribed solution that fits all industries, products, and production lines, the SMED concept encourages the critical examination of line change procedures and focuses waste elimination efforts on the processes that surround production and not just the production line itself.

In addition to the obvious reduction in changeover time, a host of other benefits are associated with proper implementation of SMED.

- Even if the number of changeovers increases, machine work rates still increase due to the reduction in setup times (net gain).
- Standardized and accurate setup eliminates defective production due to setup error.
- Defect rate is also decreased due to the decreased need for trial runs and calibrating runs.
- Quality is improved due to fully regulated operating conditions in advance (machines "hit the ground running" and require less tweaking).
- Simpler setups improve safe working conditions and necessitate fewer tools/labor costs.

The key benefit, however, remains the ability to respond to changes in production needs quickly and flexibly without incurring prohibitive amounts of cost and thus losing competitive edge.

While the specifics of successful SMED implementation vary from production line to production line, the key is to differentiate internal setup operations from external ones. Internal setup operations are those that require the complete shutdown of machines; internal setup operations stop production by halting the line. External setup operations are those that can, and should, be completed while the machine is running. External setup operations can be performed without any impact on production; the machine keeps running and the line keeps moving.

When implementing SMED methods across the production processes, decision makers should attempt to convert as many internal setup operations as possible into external ones instead. While this may not necessarily reduce the actual setup time in terms of minutes, it does reduce the impact of changeovers on the production line through the ability to make changes "on the fly."

Just-In-Time

Just-In-Time is a production and inventory control strategy designed to reduce costs through reductions in on-hand inventory. The overriding theory behind JIT is simple: the carrying costs associated with the storage of unused inventory are a waste of resources. The JIT philosophy itself is a combination of statistics, behavioral science, management, industrial engineering, and production management. These disciplines have come together to redefine how inventory relates to management and how it is defined on the business level.

JIT uses the carrying costs associated with inventory to expose issues with manufacturing or excess production. The idea is that removing inventory exposes preexisting manufacturing issues, and a focus on reducing on-hand inventory will not only expose these issues but preempt them in the efforts to constantly improve these protocols and procedures. This means that firms are pushed to not only require fewer inventories but to *generate* fewer inventories and to avoid waste events related to inventory.

The overall focus of JIT can be summed up as the need to have "the right material at the right time at the right place in the exact right amount to fulfill business needs." This, in practice, will reduce the generation of wasteful safety stock, because an inventory safety net is not necessary. This is not an overnight change for many firms; the traditional methods are still strong with many corporations.

In these circumstances, in which traditional methods reign supreme, a gradual reduction is necessary. JIT requires sophisticated levels of cooperation and communication between suppliers and buyers to coordinate delivery and production, so it is not a cost-effective solution for some organizations. In many cases relationships between members of a supply chain network need to be improved before Just-In-Time production and inventory can be implemented.

To Recap

- The Lean production system relies on the concept of a pull production system. Using this system of production, actual customer demand "pulls" materials and finished goods through the production process. This approach is much more responsive, flexible, and efficient than traditional "push" models of production that rely on forecasted demand and large batch sizes with long and costly line changes.

- SIPOC maps are a variant of process maps that display critical information regarding a process in the areas of suppliers, inputs, process data, outputs, and customers. Still another variant of a process map is a spaghetti plot. A spaghetti plot is a visual record of the paths that things (these things could be people, materials, or finished goods) travel throughout a space. Spaghetti plots represent physical flow and movement; they are valuable tools for decision makers and process designers.

- Value stream mapping is a much more complicated and comprehensive process mapping tool. Here a process is examined in a detailed overview that incorporates all of the process inputs. Value stream mapping should not be undertaken lightly; the process is expensive and complicated, though the end result is an invaluable waste identification tool.

- To build a foundation from which the successes of Lean can be launched, the 5S method is a set of prescribed workplace and staffing activities that maintain a productive and efficient environment. Standing for sort, segregate, shine, standardize, and self-discipline, these foundational methods are essential components of the Lean system and serve as a springboard within the world of Lean Six Sigma.

- Concrete metrics that can be used to determine if a process suffers from high waste are helpful to decision makers and systems planners. These simple but powerful tools—PCE, Little's Law, and Workstation Turnover—can be a fast indicator of the effects of innovation.

- Covering all of the production bases, Lean and, by extension, Lean Six Sigma rely on the total productive maintenance process to ensure that production isn't interrupted by unexpected line stoppages due to equipment defects. TPM also prescribes a preventative maintenance plan that should be implemented by organizations that rely heavily on machines or mechanical equipment in their business activities.

- Rapid setup (SMED—single minute exchange of die) is the driving force behind the pull production system in the sense that the fast line changes that it fosters are essential to keep pull production fast, flexible, and responsive.

- Keeping inventory costs and lead times low, Just-In-Time is an inventory control method that uses coordinated scheduling to move exact amounts of goods to the exactly correct time and place; this way less have to be kept on hand.

Key Questions (answers on pg. 171)

1. The pull production system method of manufacture seeks to alleviate which of the following challenges normally associated with traditional push methods?

   a) long line downtimes due to line changeovers

   b) buffer inventory and surplus stock to correct for demand fluctuations

   c) large, inflexible batch sizes

   d) all of the above

2. Process mapping should be done as a business activity and offers no additional value.

   a) true

   b) false

3. SIPOC is which of the following?

   a) service, infrastructure, process, overtime, customers

   b) suppliers, inputs, process, outputs, customers

   c) suppliers, infrastructure, process, outputs, customers

   d) SIPOC is none of the above

4. Which of the following best describes the process of value stream mapping?

a) a complex mapping process that displays all inputs for a process

b) a low-cost method of understanding customer needs

c) an independent audit of a production facility

d) a mapping process for administrative functions

5. Which of the following is not an element of the 5S method?

a) sort

b) segregate

c) select

d) standardize

6. When calculating the time-based metric PCE (process cycle efficiency), which of the following best describes process lead time?

a) a scheduled period of production

b) the amount of time in a process that is committed to adding value

c) a calculated value derived from a process map

d) a calculated value reached using Little's Law

7. Total productive maintenance (TPM) is a structured and comprehensive program designed to accomplish which of the following?

a) reduce unscheduled downtime due to equipment failure

b) increase scheduled downtime so that it can be better planned for

c) increase production staff competency in process functions

d) better match product offerings with customer needs

8. Rapid setup methods are beneficial to the production process in which of the following ways?

a) an increase in production flexibility

b) shorter line changeover times

c) a decrease in batch sizes resulting in less inventory

d) all of the above

| 5 |

The Hybrid Approach : Lean Six Sigma

In This Chapter

- The critical concept of VOC (Voice of the Customer) is detailed, including customer segmentation
- Samples of tools are presented to assist in the VOC data collection process and the critical-to-quality requirements planning process
- Complexity of operations and the complexity equation are demonstrated
- Various cause-and-effect investigative methods are explored

Drawing from the efficiency and waste reduction methods that Lean provides and the statistically-driven quality-improvement approaches that Six Sigma offers, a "best practices" program is born. While the component philosophies are distinct, their natures complement one another. Many of the tools in each toolbox can be intermingled, and firms adopting Lean Six Sigma have the ability to pick and choose which methods are most appropriate for their businesses.

It is important to note that adopting Lean Six Sigma is not the same as adopting both Lean and Six Sigma programs simultaneously. The aim of the hybrid approach is to select complementary tools and methods that work in unison to produce the best results for the business. Many tools, such as PDCA and the 5 Whys method, are universally applicable and are appropriate in nearly every industry. Kaizen, too, is a powerful corporate culture mindset that effects change within an organization. What follows is a summary of the common core of both the Lean and Six Sigma programs. This core serves as a foundation upon which organizations can build their Lean Six Sigma program, and is augmented by the specific tools and processes that were covered in the preceding sections.

As we have seen, Six Sigma is a powerful and comprehensive system that leverages statistical analysis. Six Sigma provides the methods by which decision makers can evaluate their processes and the states of their production or business operations. Six Sigma doesn't offer a lot of guidance in the way of production methodology, though—in fact, nearly none. That is the world of Lean production, the standardized and highly focused production guidelines, best practices, and methodologies.

Together, the DMAIC process and kaizen culture produce an environment that encourages change and craves improvement. In a crowded marketplace where competitive edge is key, this is critical to organizational longevity and success.

fig. 41

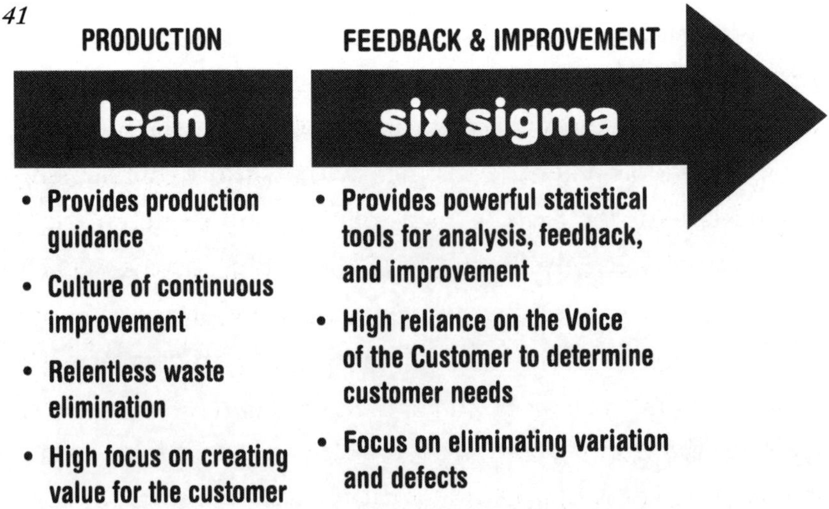

PRODUCTION

FEEDBACK & IMPROVEMENT

lean

six sigma

- Provides production guidance
- Culture of continuous improvement
- Relentless waste elimination
- High focus on creating value for the customer

- Provides powerful statistical tools for analysis, feedback, and improvement
- High reliance on the Voice of the Customer to determine customer needs
- Focus on eliminating variation and defects

While both systems—Lean and Six Sigma—straddle the line of production and feedback, decision makers for organizations that have implemented Lean Six Sigma play to the strengths of the system and the ways that it interacts with their business or industry.

fig. 42

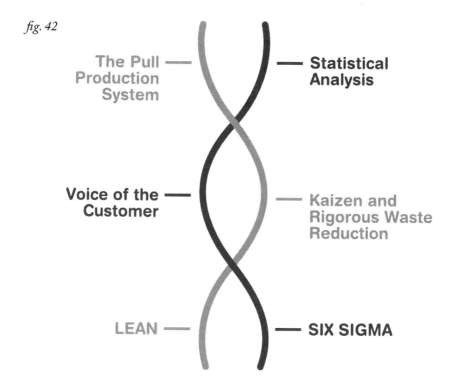

The Pull Production System — — Statistical Analysis

Voice of the Customer — — Kaizen and Rigorous Waste Reduction

LEAN — — SIX SIGMA

Voice of the Customer (VOC)

One of the key aspects of the Lean Six Sigma program is its customer-centric nature. This is more than just lip service; Lean Six Sigma prescribes rigorous methods for collecting and leveraging the *Voice of the Customer.*

The Lean method identifies production that does not add value as waste, and it centers every productive effort on demand. Six Sigma uses a method known as Voice of the Customer, and when used in conjunction with Lean's focused approach, the customer-centric effects are magnified—the hybrid program embodies that mutual focus from the very start of operations to the very end.

Using VOC data as a basis for decision making across the board ensures that corporate goals are in line with the direction of the market, and that the needs of the customer remain at the center of production or service administration.

VOC data is therefore useful in determining what customers care about when it comes to the specifications of the products they want to purchase. Once their needs have been identified, they can be met by the organization's products or services. VOC data can also be used to determine which customer needs can be met profitably and can assist decision makers in making the right business choices.

It is important to remember that not all customers are created equal; some will provide more value for the organization than others. Identifying these customers and prioritizing their needs is done through a process known as customer segmentation.

Customer Segmentation

Customer segmentation is not a concept unique to the Lean Six Sigma methodology. For years, marketing firms have been striving to better understand customer needs and the conditions that affect their buying decisions and have been categorizing them based on this data.

Customer segmentation is a tool that can be used to augment the design or improvement process by identifying the groups or subgroups of customers that offer the most value to the organization and understanding their needs. As with every process within the Lean Six Sigma framework, the first step is to define the output being studied, or segmented for. This output may be a product or a service.

Once the output has been defined, the improvement team brainstorms the characteristics of customers that are a good fit for that output based on existing data, market data, and best judgment. These broad categories are refined through another round of brainstorming that focuses on the characteristics that define the segmentation groups and how they may interact with the defined output and the organization. At this stage it is best to focus on just a few characteristics.

Decision makers can now build profiles for different customer segments. These could be profiles based on region, age, gender, income, or any other relevant factor—for example, homeowners with children vs. homeowners with no children.

The purpose of these activities is to refine the actual VOC data collection process that can consist of any one of (better, a mix of) the following methods:

Interviews

Interviews are a method of establishing dialogue with *individual* customers that allows designers and improvement team members to take a deep look into the ways in which specific customers use their product or service. While interviews tend to be fairly structured, there is room for flexibility to explore topics dynamically.

It would be a costly endeavor for a B2C (business to consumer) organization to interview each of its customers on a one-on-one basis, so this method of VOC data gathering is often best applied to a B2B (business to business) customer via a contact point or organizational representative, although interviews don't have to be strictly one-on-one scenarios.

When used at the beginning of a project in the design phase, interviews can help designers understand customer expectations and needs. These insights will either prop up or tear down preconceived brainstormed data, and the appropriate follow-up action should be taken.

When used in the middle of a project or design phase, interviews can be used to clarify specific items or to leverage customers as sounding boards for proposed ideas or product/service enhancements.

When used at the end of a project or design phase, interviews can act as vital feedback that will either confirm improvement or encourage a second look on the part of decision makers.

Point-of-Use Observation

Point-of-use observation is the viewing and recording of customers using or consuming your product or service. This could be as complicated as receiving permission to observe corporate customers putting your outputs to use, or as simple as setting up a booth in a retail store.

In each circumstance, the objective is the same: to glean valuable information about customer experience and interaction with outputs and the brand itself. The specifics of this process vary between the nature of the output (product or service) and the nature of the customers (business or consumer), but there are several guidelines that should be followed to produce actionable results.

- Define the purpose of the observation.
- Define the conditions under which the observation will take place (when, where, how).
- Construct and test a data collection form.
- Train data collectors/observers.
- Run the observation as a pilot with low-impact customers to debug the process.
- Conduct the observation and perform data analysis.

Focus Groups

Focus Groups fill the same role as interviews in the sense that they can support a wider variety of questions and encourage more in-depth answers than surveys, but they are much more cost-effective than individual interviews. Additionally, collective discussion can be much more productive than the input of an individual customer.

Focus group data collecting can also be used in conjunction with surveys as a follow-up or pre-survey collection method, or can be blended with interview style follow-ups from a dedicated focus group.

Focus groups are often comprised of between seven and thirteen members, and the general rule is that the more groups that provide data, the more comprehensive the VOC data collecting activity will be. Resources such as time and budgetary concerns will ultimately limit the number of focus groups that can be utilized but under no circumstances should just one focus group's data be relied upon. The same open-ended environment that breeds exploration and actionable information can also create skewed data due to the less-structured decisions.

Focus groups can be made up of members of a single customer segment, or they can be made up of a mix of customers from across a number of segments. Once participants have been identified, questions can be developed and piloted to determine their effectiveness at guiding the conversation and providing helpful results.

The actual conducting of a focus group is easier said than done, and if there is no one within the organization who is competent or qualified, there are nearly endless numbers of organizations who specialize in market data and sampling who will be able to conduct the focus group VOC data collection on the organization's behalf.

Surveys

Surveys are the least expensive, and least comprehensive, method of collecting VOC data. Often used to greatest effect when combined with other methods of VOC data collection such as focus groups, surveys offer a structured and focused approach to gathering potentially massive amounts of customer opinion data from an entire group or customer segment.

Additionally, while the other three methods of VOC data collection have involved mostly qualitative data, surveys offer highly actionable data in the form of quantitative data results—this makes surveys particularly well suited as pre-work or follow-up collection methods for focus groups or interviews.

When utilizing surveys, the first step is, of course, to define the objectives of the survey. Once that is complete, determine an appropriate sample size based on objectives and budget. When developing the survey's questions and makeup, keep in mind that the data from numerical scales is much easier to process, such as a rating system of one through five. Analyze each question; does the information gathered from that question meet the defined objectives of the survey? If not, adjust.

Just like the other VOC data collection methods, conducting a pilot program can help debug the process before the surveys are deployed en masse.

Many of the VOC data collection activities will fall under the purview of the sales and marketing departments at most organizations, but it is important for decision makers in both those departments and the production departments to collaborate (Lean, visibility) and ensure that collection is carried out in a statistically sound manner and is collected to spec using standardized collection techniques.

fig. 43

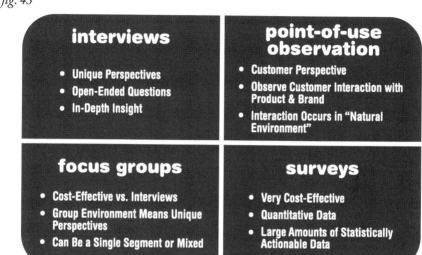

From these distinctions it is evident that no single method of data collection will paint the whole picture. It is unwise for organizations to rely on only a single method of VOC data collection. We know that VOC data informs designers and decision makers of customers' needs and requirements, but what does an organization do with that information once they have it? Should all of the customer input have the same weight, or should some specifications be elevated over others?

VOC data is used to shape the critical-to-quality requirements, the attributes and parameters that define whether a product or service meets quality requirements or is classified as a defect. Critical-to-quality requirements are central to production operations or service administration, and their importance cannot be overstated. While the Lean system of production helps Lean Six Sigma adherent organizations produce their goods in an economical and efficient way, Six Sigma guides those efforts to meeting the needs of the customer and reducing defective production through VOC data collection and the definition of robust critical-to-quality requirements.

Kano Analysis

To sort the attributes that customers value most, and the ones that will prescribe critical-to-requirement parameters, a method called a *Kano analysis* is used. The purpose of this refining process is to determine customer requirements as they relate to deliverables—these can help shape critical-to-quality requirements in the future. A Kano analysis can also provide insight into customer needs that were not explicitly stated, or can help designers and decision makers identify characteristics included in previous offerings that may still be valued by the customer.

A Kano analysis should be used when defining or measuring the scope and importance of project goals, or when redesigning a product, service, or business process. To begin, VOC data should be collected (through more than one means of collection, such as interviews, focus groups, *and* surveys), and known existing customer needs should be listed.

These needs are then presented to the customer framed as questions with one of four answers indicating expectations and interest.

- How would the customer feel if the need or feature was met? This is a positive fulfillment.

- How would the customer feel if the need or feature wasn't met? This is a negative fulfillment.

Their answers are based on one of four options:

1. I'd like it
2. It is normally that way (the fulfillment of this need or feature is expected)
3. I don't care
4. I wouldn't like it

These answers to the two types of fulfillment questions generate a chart that displays the results.

Answers to Negative Questions

	like	normal	don't care	don't like
like		Delighter	Delighter	Satisfier
normal				Dissatisfier
don't care				Dissatisfier
don't like				

*(Row labels on left: **Answers to Positive Questions**)*

fig. 44: A sample Kano analysis. This matrix is used to identify satisfiers and dissatisfiers based on customer responses.

Dissatisfiers

Dissatisfiers are aspects that are considered *basic* requirements. These represent the entry-level quality of a service or product, and if these requirements are not met, then customers will be very dissatisfied. Dissatisfiers represent a minimum expectation of quality standards, and meeting the dissatisfiers is generally regarded as the entry point for a product or service's market.

It is important to note that customers will rarely name basic requirements as needs; everyone expects that a car will have wheels and a windshield. It is the responsibility of the organization to determine what the baseline level of quality and expectation is within a market and make sure that these essential standards are met first.

Satisfiers

Satisfiers are aspects that are considered *performance* requirements. These are standard characteristics that can either decrease satisfaction or increase it based on their degree and expression. These aspects include attributes such as price and ease of use. While meeting the minimum requirements (dissatisfiers) will allow an organization entry into a market, meeting performance requirements in a competitive way ensures that the organization maintains a presence in the market.

When VOC data is collected, it is satisfiers that are most often named when customers are asked to describe what is important to them. A car that requires minimal maintenance, for example, or a variety of body styles and sport or deluxe models are satisfiers for the automotive market.

Delighters

Delighters are aspects that are considered *excitement* requirements. These characteristics or features are unexpected by customers and provide increased levels of value and satisfaction. Delighters are the aspects that set organizations apart from their competitors and open the door to favorable market positioning, market dominance, and world class innovation and excellence.

Because delighters are often innovative in nature, they have never been seen before, and as such could not realistically be expected to come up in VOC data collection efforts. These aspects must be generated from a higher-level understanding of the market in which an organization operates, their business, and their customers' existing needs.

The first cars to feature voice recognition features, for example, would be classified as having features that delighted customers. While customers would expect that they could play music or integrate hands-free functionality with their vehicle, the inclusion of voice recognition and voice commands is valuable to many drivers, though not something they would have necessarily requested.

Market mobility, the meeting of basic market needs, the competitive maintaining of a market position, and the steady rise through a market, are distinct expressions of the cooperative nature of Lean Six Sigma. These factors "bring it all together" in the sense that Lean's kaizen culture and innovative focus blend with the Six Sigma methods of identifying need and defining and ensuring quality.

Critical-to-Quality Requirements

The most expensive and comprehensive VOC data collection program may still turn up a panoply of vague and less-than-descriptive qualifiers for an organization's product or service. While customers can be a wealth of data concerning their needs and expectations, in some cases they may not really know what they want. Sometimes customers take features for granted, or they can't adequately articulate their needs in a way that is useful to an organization.

Determining the critical-to-quality requirements for a process is a procedure that takes the often vague input from customers and produces refined, actionable directives.

Raw VOC data is often emotion-based, nonspecific, and vague.

- *I feel like I'm not getting a good value.*
- *This is a good product that functions well.*
- *I wish there was more functionality.*

It may take several follow-up or investigative approaches on the part of the data collection team to ascertain the true motives for these statements. A deeper dive might turn up the root causes of the feelings expressed.

- *I feel like I'm not getting a good value because the price of the product is not competitive.*
- *This product functions well because it is durable and performs as advertised.*
- *I wish there was more functionality in the areas of connectivity and cross-platform compatibility.*

While these expanded statements are more descriptive of how customers perceive the product and what their expectations are, they are still not actionable and do not reflect quantifiable targets.

- *I feel like I'm not getting a good value because the price of the product is not competitive. It is higher than a comparable product by nearly 20 percent.*

- *This product functions well because it is durable and performs as advertised. It has a stated lifespan of three years or 30,000 cycles, and it has met or exceeded that lifespan.*

- *I wish there was more functionality in the areas of connectivity and cross-platform compatibility. I manage a team of developers from all over the globe, and your product does not allow for a very streamlined remote collaboration experience.*

These results have explored the underlying reasons for the customer expectations and represent actionable information that can be turned into goals.

fig. 45

initial statement	underlying cause	key attribute	refined goal
"I feel like I'm not getting a good value."	Price-Related Concerns	Price is higher than the competition by 20%	Reduce price to customer by *at least* 20%
"This is a good product that functions well."	Feature-Related	Lasts for entire lifespan	Maintain lifespan of 3 years/30,000 cycles
"I wish there was more functionality."	Feature-Related Concerns	Cannot easily collaborate with other users worldwide	Increase global compatibility and match product to popular platforms

Useful goals will conform to the following criteria:

- Actionable goals are easily measured (quantifiable) and specific.
- Actionable goals are related directly to a specific attribute of the product or service.
- Actionable goals are bias free and do not offer alternative paths to completion. Bias toward a particular approach is a limiting factor that can reduce the effects of efforts to innovate by stifling the creative process.
- Actionable goals do not prescribe a method for meeting goals, but instead merely describe how a need will be met.

Complexity of Operations

Many of the tools in the Lean and Six Sigma toolkits are designed to address waste and variation within a single product or system. While this narrow focus means that each one of the products or systems identified are thoroughly investigated and dissected, the challenge of identifying and tackling business operations with elevated levels of complexity often remains out of reach.

Product/Service Family Grid

A *product family grid* (or service family grid) is a visual tool that classifies a variety of processes or products into "families" or similar process steps or characteristics. A product grid is an essential first step in the complexity analysis process—it lays the groundwork and the parameters for the majority of the analysis efforts that follow.

The sample product grid below returns to the example of an ice cream shop. Products (ice cream cones and sundaes) are classified into families based on their ingredients and process steps.

fig. 46

	Process Steps/Ingredients							
	cone	waffle cone	dish	soft serve machine	regular ice cream	hot fudge	sprinkles	family
Soft Serve Cone	X			X				A
Soft Serve Dish			X	X				B
Regular Cone	X				X			A
Regular Dish			X		X			B
Soft Serve Waffle		X		X				C
Regular Waffle		X			X			C
Sundae			X		X	X	X	D
Dip Cone	X				X	X	X	A
Dip Waffle		X			X	X	X	B

The specific criteria that are used to determine which aspects of a process classify it into a family depend on the subprocesses that make up each product or service, and on the business in question.

The Complexity Equation

The complexity equation is an investigative application of the process cycle efficiency equation. It is used to identify steps in a process that are falling short of expected PCE levels.

The following equation is a general representation of the complexity equation. Organizations applying this formula in practice will need to insert a number of additional variables, though these variables will vary from industry to industry and from process to process.

fig. 47

$$PCE = \frac{2V(1 - x - PD)}{N(2S + 1)S}$$

Where:

V = total value-added time

X = percent of products/services with quality defects

P = processing time per unit

D = demand for products/services

N = the number of tasks performed per activity

A = the number of activities/steps in the process

S = the longest setup time in the process

This equation is important because it forms the basis for the next level of understanding complexity within a process. PCED, or PCE Destruction, is a process by which single variables within the above equation are singled out and analyzed. The equation essentially tests for the potential conditions if a particular variable was removed.

fig. 48

$$PCED = \frac{\dfrac{\text{PCE of all steps except target - (PCE baseline)}}{\text{PCE baseline}}(100)}{\text{demand}}$$

The result of this equation is a ratio or percentage that compares the PCE with the targeted step or process (the standard complex PCE equation), and the PCE of the targeted step or process alone (again, the standard complex PCE equation) with a baseline PCE, resulting in three calculations.

fig. 49

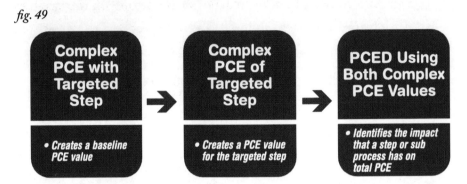

Cause & Effect

Simply knowing that there is variation or defective production is not enough; decision makers must also have investigative methods to uncover the root causes of issues so that they can be resolved through corrective action.

It is important to investigate until the root cause or underlying conditions that produced the issue are discovered. Visibility leads to action, and efforts that fail to reach the true cause of issues will only provide temporary alleviation. Investigators attempting to determine the causes of process issues are by no means restricted to the use of a single cause-and-effect tool—the more thorough the investigation, the more insight the findings will produce. This means that multiple tools should be used together to produce findings from a variety of angles.

5 Whys

The *5 Whys* method is a cause-and-effect-seeking technique that explores the root causes of a problem. Using this investigative method, each question forms the basis for the subsequent question. The first step of the 5 Whys method is to identify the problem.

In the following example, the problem is that is growing in a storeroom of perishable goods. The 5 Whys process is applied to determine the root cause. It is important to note that the solution may be determined in fewer than five iterations of the process. Five has been determined to be the average number of why-based questions needed to reach the root cause of the issue.

Problem: Mold has been detected in a storeroom housing perishable goods.

Why 1:   Why is mold growing in this room?
- *There is an excessive amount of moisture.*

Why 2:   Why is there an excessive amount of moisture?
- *There is a pool of water on the floor.*

Why 3:   Why is there a pool of water on the floor?
- *There is a hole in the ceiling of the storeroom.*

Why 4:   Why is there a hole in the ceiling of the storeroom?
- *A portion of the roof above it is sagging. Rainwater has collected in this area and created a crack in the roofing material.*

Why 5:   Why did the crack go undetected?
- *The building has not been inspected for over a decade.*

Based on this example we can see that the root cause of mold growth in the storeroom is the deterioration of the surrounding structure. The investigation also yielded the information that regular inspections of the building and its roof would have detected the source of the problem. This is a simple example, but it serves to demonstrate the effectiveness of the 5 Whys method in identifying the underlying sources of problems and defects.

The 5 Whys method is not a stand-alone approach to cause-and-effect analysis. Often, when using more complex cause-and-effect approaches, the 5 Whys process will be applied to smaller, less complex elements. While it may seem as if simply asking the same question over again is too simple to produce truly effective results, consider this: what if every tool was as easy to use and had as outsized an effectiveness as the 5 Whys method?

Fishbone Diagram

The versatile cause-and-effect diagrams developed by Kaoru Ishikawa are commonly known as *fishbone diagrams* or herringbone diagrams because of their distinctive repeating chevron shape. Ishikawa diagrams are generally suited to the process of identifying factors contributing to an overall effect, and that effect can be as large as the macro scale or as small as the micro.

Kaoru Ishikawa first developed the fishbone diagram in the 1960s as part of a trailblazing quality control program while he was with the now-famous manufacturer Kawasaki. Though fishbone diagrams were not a product of the Toyota Production System per se, they were rapidly adopted and are now a commonplace tool in the Lean practitioner's toolkit.

More distinct applications find the Ishikawa diagram in use with the processes of product design diagramming and quality defect prevention. As you will see, the construction and implementation of an effective fishbone diagram can be a time-consuming process. Multiple rounds of brainstorming and investigation should be planned and deployed carefully. When the root causes of a problem are fairly clear—machine inefficiency due to poor maintenance protocols, for example—a fishbone diagram is completely unnecessary and would cause more harm than good.

Fishbone diagrams are best used to disrupt a team's thinking and add a structured approach to a complex problem-solving process. When it seems like personnel are spinning their wheels tackling a complex effect on operations, that's when a fishbone diagram can be of most use.

Foundationally, the Ishikawa diagram groups together contributing factors or causes into categories that take a variety of production aspects into consideration. Known as the *5M's* of manufacturing, the primary causal categories are as follows:

Machine
The *machine* category encompasses any equipment related to the process or needed to accomplish the job. This includes computer systems, production tools, methods of conveyance, etc.

Method
Methods are defined as the specific protocols that govern a process or operation. This could be as tangible as production specs, or as intangible as departmental policy. Even organizational policy could have a trickledown effect on day-to-day operations, so the methodology category can be complex to evaluate.

Material

Materials include all of the material aspects associated with a process. Raw materials, work in progress, and finished goods are obvious for the manufacturing sector, but less obvious are finishing materials, fasteners, and other ancillary components. Supplies and inventories should also be considered under the heading of materials.

Manpower

Manpower encompasses every person involved in the process, from the sets of hands on the production line to foremen, supervisors, management, and beyond if applicable. Contractors—though not employees—may still have a hand in the factors that bring about a certain effect, so they should not be left out of the equation. Likewise, critical staff from suppliers and customers can have an effect on an organization's operations. While recourse or corrective action may be limited in these cases, understanding the source of an impact means that decision makers aren't entirely powerless.

Measurement

Measurement describes the total of the data that is generated from or about the process. This not only includes normal, day-to-day business metrics, but monitoring and inspection-generated data as well. Data is only as accurate as the means by which it was gathered. A critical look at the tools and systems by which the data that is used in decision making is an essential part of understanding the underlying causes of discrete effects without potential distortion as a remedy to issues caused by measurement factors.

It is worth mentioning that there is another widely recognized broad category that may be factored into causal classification: environment. Environment constitutes aspects such as temperature, geographic location, cultural norms, and all other miscellaneous aspects of production. Some interpretations of the 5Ms include as many as eight general cause categories, but the prevailing theory is that sticking to the basics is a safer and simpler approach.

The proposed causes of an effect are determined through a series of brainstorming sessions and through rigorous investigation. If a cause is determined that is unique to an industry or organization and that defies classification as one of the 5Ms of manufacturing, that does *not* mean that it is invalid.

Adaptability and flexibility are core components of the Lean Six Sigma philosophy; industry leaders that truly understand these concepts should never shy away from repurposing the Lean toolkit to fit the needs of their business. In this respect, the 5W method can be particularly helpful in determining the root cause of a problem and shaping a fishbone diagram to fit the needs of the business.

fig. 50

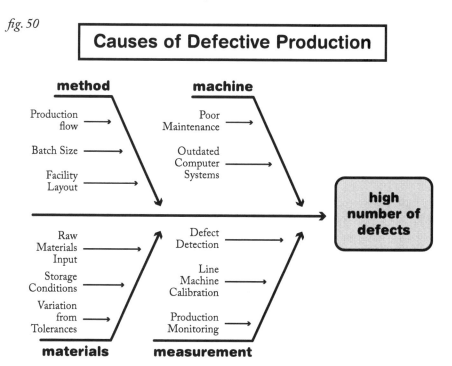

If a sixth category, environment, is appropriate for a particular industry or organization, then those fishbone diagrams should include an environment category. The same would be true if decision makers determine that there is a real need for seven or eight categories.

ANOVA

ANOVA is an acronym that stands for <u>AN</u>nalysis <u>O</u>f <u>VA</u>riables. It is a method that has wide statistical applications but can also be used to check the validity of cause-and-effect investigations and results. ANOVA testing is the comparison of three or more data samples to one another to determine if there is a statistically sound difference between the means of each.

ANOVA testing is used during the Analyze and Improve stages of DMAIC; when analyzing it is used to determine the impact of variables. When used as a part of improvement activities, it can guide decision makers in selecting the right choice from a number of alternatives.

ANOVA stands out from the cause-and-effect tools listed thus far. The 5 Whys method and fishbone chart rely on insight and the human factor to a large degree. ANOVA, on the other hand, exists almost exclusively in the world of computer-crunched numerical and statistical output. Ultimately, a human operator or decision maker will use the insights provided from an ANOVA analysis, but the procedure itself is largely done by a computer.

Within the world of statistical analysis, inputs may be referred to as factors, and the circumstances under which samples are collected, and the sources from which they are collected, are often called levels. We'll use those conventions in our discussion of ANOVA. For example, decision makers may be comparing the duration of calls from terminals A, B, and C. The calls are the factor, the "thing" being measured, while the separate terminals A, B, and C are the levels.

To determine statistically significant differences, the ANOVA method examines three aspects of variability.

Total – this is the total variability between all observations

Between – variation between subgroup means (the averages of the component levels)

Within – random variation within a subgroup, often considered noise or statistical error

What this means for decision makers is that differences are assessed in a way that tells them if differences are significant or not. They know there are differences (otherwise there would be no need for an ANOVA test); this procedure helps them identify the degree of difference between multiple data sets simultaneously.

ANOVA techniques are broadly categorized into two groups: one-way ANOVA and two-way ANOVA.

Note : It should be noted that an ANOVA is the output of a statistical software program such as Minitab and is not something that will be performed by hand or with a paper and pen.

A one-way ANOVA test determines if the mean of one result is statistically different from any others in a set. This method involves only one factor. When conducting an ANOVA test, the first steps are to define the factors, levels, and sample size. Once the data has been gathered and the ANOVA program has been run, it is often necessary to conduct a pairwise comparison. ANOVA tests tell decision makers whether or not there are statistical variations, but they do not identify which outcomes are different from alternatives. *Tukey's Pairwise Comparison* is another statistical software function and would not normally be completed by hand. Expressed as a succinct formula, Tukey's pairwise comparison is shown below:

fig. 51

$$\mu_i - \mu_j$$

In this instance, the statistical analysis software is comparing all the values in each set, $\mu_1 - \mu_2$, $\mu_1 - \mu_3$, etc., to identify the precise source of variation. A complete exploration of the theory and statistical basis of Tukey's pairwise comparison is beyond the scope of this text.

When conducting a two-way ANOVA test, multiple factors and levels may be used, though the statistical basis for the calculation is significantly more complicated.

Note : Mr. Tukey is also the statistical mind behind the box plot.

To Recap

- To determine the all-important critical-to-quality requirements, the needs of the customer must be determined and reduced to actionable goals that can inform the production process. Who better to communicate their needs than the customers themselves? Once they have been segmented into groups, customer needs, specifications, and preferences are gathered through means known as the Voice of the Customer.

- VOC data collection consists of a number of collection methods including interviews, point-of-use observation, focus groups, and surveys. VOC data that has been collected through these means can be organized through a Kano analysis, a grid-style chart that prioritizes customer expectations and needs.

- The goal of VOC data collection is to collect sufficient amounts of information from customers to create the critical-to-quality requirements that inform the production process. These efforts are in line with the overarching concepts of the "Define" step in Lean Six Sigma's DMAIC improvement process.

- When examining the complexity of operations, creating a product/service family grid is a key first step. This chart classifies various business processes based on their subprocess steps. Once this has been completed, a number of other complexity-related calculations can be performed, such as the complex PCE (process cycle efficiency) calculation and PCED (process cycle efficiency destruction) calculation, the latter of which is used to identify the contribution of specific variables to a baseline PCE.

- The 5 Whys system is a simple yet powerful structured approach to the systematic investigation of root causes. By probing the conclusions reached in each iteration of the process, the true underlying causes of issues can be exposed.

- Another, more visual method is the fishbone diagram. Borrowed from the Lean production system, it is a diagram that analyzes all of the input into a process. Categorizing and analyzing the input in a structured way contributes positively to ease of understanding and thorough investigation.

- A variable identification method that examines one or more sets of data to determine statistical differences, known as ANOVA, can be used as an investigative cause-and-effect tool. Run through statistical software such as Minitab, ANOVA analysis determines whether or not significant variation is present, but not which data values are varying.

- To locate the specific sources of variation, a Tukey's pairwise comparison must also be performed. Also the product of statistical software, a pairwise comparison checks each data point against the others to identify the specific sources of variation as data points.

Key Questions (answers on pg. 171)

1. Which of the following VOC data collection methods can be used to gather quantifiable data instead of qualitative?

   a) focus groups   b) surveys

   c) point-of-use-observations   d) interviews

2. Surveys should be used alone when gathering VOC data.

   a) true   b) false

3. Which of the following best describes critical-to-quality requirements?

   a) the total value-added time   c) the determining criteria in
      within a process   judging process inputs

   b) the standard deviation of   d) the parameters of a
      a process from its   process that indicate
      intended result   which production outputs
                                          meet customer specs and
                                          which do not

4. The PCED equation is best suited to determine which characteristic of a process?

a) adherence to customer specs

b) the role that a subprocess has in contributing to PCE

c) identifying areas where staff may be better implemented to reduce waste

d) identifying the Voice of the Customer

5. Why is a pairwise comparison a necessary follow-up to an ANOVA analysis?

a) because ANOVA analyses don't account for variation

b) because ANOVA analyses are inconclusive

c) because ANOVA analyses don't identify specific data points of variation

d) pairwise comparisons aren't necessary when performing ANOVA analyses

| 6 |

Lean Six Sigma Implementation

In This Chapter

- The path to implementation is detailed in a step-by-step process

Like any organizational culture and toolset shift, the change to Lean Six Sigma doesn't happen overnight. Before any of the other steps can be initiated, decision makers at the organizational level must have a need for the Lean Six Sigma program. There must be a business imperative and a business case for the adoption of the Lean Six Sigma program.

The best cases are the ones that are grounded in facts; a statement such as "the losses due to poor quality have exceeded 30 percent of our total loss portfolio, and we need to rectify this right away" is representative of exactly the kind of scenario that Lean Six Sigma is equipped to handle.

Knowing *why* Lean Six Sigma is important to the organization is a huge driver in uniform, motivated, and ultimately successful adoption, especially if the reasons are related to significant losses due to quality or competitor gains in market share.

Once the business case has been established for the adoption of Lean Six Sigma, then the broad strokes of the implementation and adoption process can begin.

1. Use Resources

There is a wealth of comprehensive—albeit expensive—training resources that are available to expedite the adoption and implementation process for motivated organizations. Coaches, gurus, and Lean Six

Sigma experts are the best and fastest way to put the power of Lean Six Sigma into effect for an organization. Additionally, the learning curve is shortened considerably when a Lean Six Sigma coach can provide best practices to the organization and circumvent costly learning through trial and error.

The value of quality Lean Six Sigma coaches and mentors cannot be overstated. These are the people who are not only effecting the change within the organization on the interpersonal level, but, as a result, along the entire org chart. While the success of adoption relies on many aspects, empowering agents of organizational change is a key part of a successful adoption process.

2. Teach & Adhere to the Methodology

There are reasons why programs like Lean and Six Sigma have been more than just a flash in the pan. The systems' designers ensured that by codifying everything as either a process or a component of the methodology's culture, the entire system benefited from the economies of repetition and familiarity that the "total organizational commitment" approach offers.

This means commitments at all levels to the culture of kaizen and an integration of the organization's existing org chart into the Six Sigma colored belt ranking system. Here, coaches, mentors, and external trainers can have a tremendous effect on the motivation and involvement of employees. Staff commitment is absolutely essential to the success of implementation and to smooth adoption. Those team members who are selected to set the example and lead the charge should be wholly committed to the organization's vision and to the case for change.

3. Focus on Priorities

With such sweeping changes across the organization it can be easy for decision makers to get overwhelmed and focus on the wrong activities for success. Before, during, and after the adoption process decision makers and members of the management team should focus on priorities.

- Listen to the customer
- Identify critical-to-quality requirements
- Ensure that Lean Six Sigma efforts are aligned with business goals

These criteria are broad, and intentionally so. Lean Six Sigma has a wide range of applications across a number of industries. Decision makers are always going to be tweaking their application of the methodology to their specific business, but some things are absolutes across the board.

Listening to the customer has been established time and time again in nearly every modern business guidance program as an absolutely crucial element of success. Lean focuses on value and the creation of utility for the customer based on customer specs. Six Sigma's VOC data collection methods inform those same customer specs. There is no reason to disconnect these two business functions once they have been connected. Listening to the customer should be the highest priority of production and business activities.

The insights gained from customers are distilled into the critical-to-quality requirements that create actionable goals for business operations. These are the parameters that define production and business activities. These activities should always be linked and in line with overall business goals and priorities so that organizational expectations can be met.

fig. 52

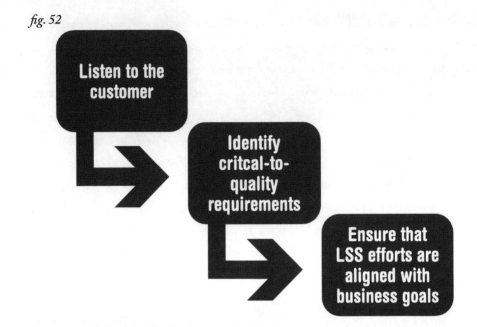

4. Establish Key Ownership

Total organizational commitment is essential for a smooth adoption of Lean Six Sigma, and ownership of new business initiatives generates pride, commitment, and engagement among management and frontline staff alike. Accountability is a large portion of any committed business activity, and that is no less true when it comes to the top-to-bottom restricting that accompanies the Lean Six Sigma adoption process.

When so many organizations claim that their most valuable asset is their people, the aspects of Lean Six Sigma—particularly from the Lean component—rely on competent, accountable, and engaged staff in new ways. While every organization wants dedicated personnel who share in the organizational vision, never before has it been as relevant or necessary than when making the leap to Lean Six Sigma.

5. Make the Measurements Count

Because so much of the Lean Six Sigma program relies on measurement and analysis, it is extremely important that the right metrics are recorded and that the right data is collected. This means that data collection methods and protocol should be regularly examined to ensure that the data that is being collected is *the right data*.

The right data is data that is helpful, actionable, and informative. The right data will inform decisions in a helpful way and identify relevant trends, metrics, and determining factors; while the Lean Six Sigma protocol does prescribe some factors to take into account, these are by no means a one-size-fits-all recommendation. Organizations must mold the Lean Six Sigma program to their field or industry, not the other way around.

The data collected must represent the true costs of quality, and it must represent the true amount of variation from quality. Lean teaches us that visibility leads to action, and that which has not been quantified cannot be reduced or impacted. This is not to say that everything that can be measured should be measured—determining the critical metrics and applying the learning that they convey is a key part of the Lean Six Sigma method.

6. Send Ownership up the Chain of Command

Finding the right balance of Lean Six Sigma governance is crucial to the program's success and propagation throughout an organization. Sending ownership up the chain of command is an extension of support from management; the Lean principles of visibility, flexibility, and simplicity are all foundational to implementation success, but accountability throughout the process and beyond is key.

7. Recognize Standout Efforts

The reward of contributions is a major driver of employee participation at all levels, and can generate authentic enthusiasm for success. While the decision to adopt Lean Six Sigma comes from the top down, encouragement and a willingness to recognize standout contributors to success must come down the hierarchy with it.

If this is done correctly, support will be generated from the frontline levels of the organization, and it will move up the chain of command to meet the imperatives that are being issued from the top down. Managers, decision makers, and corporate officers of all stripes understand that sweeping changes have a much higher success rate when adoption has grassroots support throughout all levels of the organization.

| 7 |
Criticism & Issues

In This Chapter

- We discuss some of the criticisms and challenges associated with the Lean Six Sigma doctrine

In assessing the practicality and viability of any management system, organizations should inspect past implementations. This does not just mean reading success stories; a thorough understanding of obstacles and pitfalls is even more instructive. There is no magic pill in the world of business. Lean Six Sigma and its component methodologies are effective tools, but like all programs, they are not without flaws.

Six Sigma

A primary point of criticism with the Six Sigma method is that while it is adept at addressing individual issues and developing low-defect systems, it is a narrowly focused, and in many cases, a reactionary tool. Six Sigma was developed to assist production and improve quality within specific processes, and it lacks a broader scope. Lean Six Sigma's hybrid approach mitigates this disadvantage with its extra focus on the value stream and VOC.

In the world of Six Sigma, another criticism arises when management professionals see the amount of time the system uses that is not devoted to normal business activities. Six Sigma requires training, which is in some cases lengthy. Additionally, master black belt and black belt-level staff spend almost all of their time immersed in the Six Sigma process. These facts are undisputed. The decision to implement Six Sigma should be addressed by an informed management group, and the staff implications as well as the possible benefits should be weighed on a case-by-case basis. Companies with limited resources may find that Six Sigma is not a viable option for their business methods or model.

A related point of criticism is the expert nature of Six Sigma. Companies seeking to adopt the program will not only need to expend staff hours on training and organization, but in many cases they will require consulting and coaching from an outside professional. Some companies are not comfortable relying on outside assistance or are unwilling to pay the premiums for the services if the need for change isn't critical. If a company attempts to implement the program without experienced guidance, they may face additional hardships during adoption or the program may fail to take hold within the organization. These issues may additionally lead to diminished returns from the system in the long run and may be the source of wasted resources and effort.

It is important to remember as well that even "white belt" members of the organization should have a basic understanding of the goals of the Six Sigma and Lean Six Sigma programs, as their statistical and empirical nature can cause apprehension among rank-and-file employees. Management, too, is not immune. The best way to overcome issues with top-to-bottom programs is to get the right information; implementers, practitioners, management, coaches, and non-participatory staff should all know their roles within the transition to Lean Six Sigma.

Six Sigma, like Lean, is arguably a poor solution for the monitoring of creative processes. While the design for Six Sigma protocol is equipped to produce new systems, the methodology is out of place in the marketing and creative components of an organization. Repeatable processes and operations that can be quantified and measured are much more appropriate candidates.

Lean

Old habits are an impediment to Lean implementation. If management discovers the root of a problem with waste and efficiency, the decision-making process is limited to the boardroom, doesn't include input from production staff, and the solution begins after far too much time has elapsed in deliberation. True visibility within an organization and commitment to the practice of kaizen would utilize the input of the frontline workforce and observe the process at the production level, not from the boardroom. These conditions result in sound decision making on paper, but solutions can fail to improve the situation or have the intended reduction result.

Additionally, practitioners of Lean tend to use the model as a "one size fits all" waste reduction program. This is usually not the case, as the specific implementation changes from application to application. While the culture of kaizen and the concepts of differentiating between value-added and non-value-added activities are powerful enough to span diverse industries, some firms simply find that not every tool is needed or even helpful. Implementation of a hybrid program that takes all of the beneficial parts of Lean and pairs them to the specific needs of the organization is the most effective use of the Lean model, as opposed to a headfirst "leap to Lean." Pairing the necessary portions of the Lean business model with the quality-centric Six Sigma program mitigates these programs further and can compound the benefits that a company sees from implementation.

A frequent criticism is that planners implementing Lean focus on the tools and qualitative methods as opposed to the culture. The Lean business model is designed to be a "total package" solution in implementation, and while the tools and methods can be effectively used piecemeal, or as a pairing with Six Sigma, the true value of Lean exists in the kaizen culture that tirelessly strives for improvement used in conjunction with the variety of Lean's other business improvement tools.

| 8 |
The Lean Six Sigma Sub-Industry

In This Chapter
- This chapter is a brief look at the Six Sigma sub-industry

Lean Six Sigma uses several statistical techniques drawn from its component methodologies. This statistical base can make the program more difficult to implement, since many employees may find statistically heavy analysis foreign. Additionally, the value-added focus of Lean is unfamiliar to some. Implementation of the system, therefore, requires training and advanced methods, the scope of which many enterprises are not equipped to achieve on their own.

The success of Lean Six Sigma has created a need for specialists in its implementation, adoption, and philosophy. These expert consultants provide advisory and training services to organizations interested in adoption. Lean Six Sigma consultants also assist in viability studies to determine if the program is a good fit for the organization. In the case of long-term adoption, the management consultant will train senior staff who in turn propagate the program throughout the organization by training subordinates.

Because of the highly scientific nature of the Lean Six Sigma program and the complexity of its business management components, professional consultants require accreditation. The International Association for Six Sigma Certification issues certificates to program participants based on their success in standardized examinations and provides consultants with the statistical and Six Sigma background necessary for enterprise-wide adoption.

At present, there are more than thirty tertiary institutions that offer Six Sigma certification programs, the bulk of which are located in the United States. In many cases implementation also requires advanced statistical software that analyzes the system and provides a framework for the tools on which Six Sigma relies. At present, there are nearly fifty programs on the market. Proprietary software is usually expensive, and the open source options are not extensive. This added cost, as well as the skills required to use the software, can be a deterrent to organizations adopting Lean Six Sigma on a long-term basis.

Literature on Lean Six Sigma, unlike that of its constituent components, remains limited. Because it is new and still somewhat contested, a large body of work exploring the matter does not yet exist. Those interested in learning more are advised not only to study the material that specifically covers Lean Six Sigma but also the older, more extensive material on the separate parent systems. Case studies regarding implementation, adoption, and obstacles within large organizations can also be instructive. Below is a list of reading material specifically aimed at Lean Six Sigma:

1. *What is Lean Six Sigma?* by Michael L. George, David Rowlands, and Bill Kastle (2003).

2. *The Lean Six Sigma Pocket Toolbook* by Michael L. George, David Rowlands, and John Maxey (2004).

3. *Lean Six Sigma for Service: How to Use Lean Speed and Six Sigma Quality to Improve Services and Transactions* by Michael L. George (2003).

4. *Taking Lean Six Sigma Beyond Manufacturing: The Journey to Business Improvement* by Cindy Jutras (2009).

5. *International Journal of Lean Six Sigma* (a quarterly publication established in 2010).

It should be noted that the third title in the above list is aimed specifically at Lean Six Sigma in the services sector. Material on the parent systems—Lean and Six Sigma—is abundant and easy to find. Literature concerning Lean Six Sigma has increased substantially since 2010, and as more organizations adopt the program, that trend will continue to grow.

In the world of management consulting there is little pro bono work; these services are neither free nor cheap. Prospective clients should assess the potential savings and revenue opportunities associated with Lean Six Sigma against the expense of contracted expertise and implementation. Six Sigma starts with measurement and analysis; if financial constraints prohibit the full implementation of the program, then those may be the only steps taken.

Management should always subscribe to the Lean Six Sigma philosophy of involving every employee, no matter how marginally, when using a consultant. As with any top-down sweeping change, those at the top should never neglect active participation. This is important for the longevity of the program, the satisfaction of the shareholders, and the morale of the workforce.

conclusion

Global technology, business philosophy, and conventional wisdom have created a surge in the development of hybrids throughout the modern marketplace. Globalization, international cooperation, and the instantaneous transfer of knowledge have contributed to the creation of expertise and products previously thought unattainable. Lean Six Sigma is the product of this mindset and this environment. The need for a durable competitive edge has never been more pressing.

Separately, the Lean and Six Sigma methods both provide solutions for companies seeking waste reduction, efficiency, and quality. Not surprisingly, the next step in improvement and creation of competitive edge is the pairing of the two programs. Companies that adopt the hybrid solution report massive levels of improvement, but the decision to change and the process of optimizing those changes is neither fast nor cheap. Process management professionals and top-level management should thoroughly research and evaluate how the Lean Six Sigma program could potentially work within their organization and their product offerings before committing to the methodology.

There is, of course, a multitude of ways to reach the next level of business performance and to preserve competitive edge and market share; Lean Six Sigma is one method in an entire sea of business improvement tactics, methodologies, and philosophies. Readers are encouraged to research the most popular alternatives to Lean Six Sigma as well. The best decision anyone can make in business, or in life, is an informed one.

appendix a
Value Stream Mapping Sample

Value stream mapping was touched on starting on page 78. The process can become quite complex and is very time-consuming. It is important to remember that effective value stream mapping requires a high degree of coordination between different workforce elements and a thorough understanding of and practical competence in the Lean methodology.

Value stream mapping is not for novice Lean enterprises. A well-developed level of trust between and among supervisors, operators, and upper management is necessary for effective and impactful value stream mapping. It is also important to keep in mind that value stream mapping—in the instances of both strategic and tactical use—may prompt decision makers to make a number of changes to processes, labor classifications, and existing layouts.

So why use a value stream map at all?

Value stream maps are first and foremost visibility and efficiency analysis tools. Areas of waste and inefficiency cannot be addressed if they are not made visible, and an effective value stream map does just that; it reveals challenges and barriers within a process or family of processes. In this capacity, a value stream map is a diagnostic tool that forms the basis of an improvement plan for a process.

Like a blueprint, decision makers can refer back to a value stream map as a sort of common language or starting point to inform their improvement endeavors. In this way, the VSM tool serves to increase the visibility and communication between different workforce elements as well; with a unified and common point of reference, collaboration is a smoother process.

Value stream maps are effective at the organizational and departmental levels for the aforementioned reasons; this macro-level visual representation also contains a snapshot of relevant metrics and a bird's-eye view of the process as a whole from start to finish. On a more micro scale they can also help individual operators, supervisors, and decision makers understand the relationships and flows of materials, labor, and information, and the work-in-progress that responds to customer demand.

When analyzing a process and identifying the goals of value stream mapping efforts, common process issues that require elimination or reduction include the following:

Excessive DOWNTIME waste such as waiting, motion, or inventory. This *muda* could be in the form of too many handoffs, unneeded approvals, or the wasteful duplication of work—all of which can be identified through the analysis of an effective value stream map. Dead zones in the process flow can also be identified. Dead zones are areas throughout the process where work gets held up or lost, or where overall process flow is disrupted. In total, any lost time, wasted effort, and other non-value-added activities become much more visible through the value stream mapping process.

VSMs are both strategic and tactical tools. When created to analyze and design an ideal "future state" of a process, the map itself is a strategic tool. Here decision makers and members of management can make a wish list of what they would like to see in the improved version of the process. Once the value stream map has been analyzed, the resulting implementation plans aiming to arrive at the ideal future state of the process are tactical tools. Based on interpretations of the data recorded in the VSM, these plans are often tailored in the micro scale.

Step 1 : Select a Product or Service Family

The product/service family grid can be a helpful tool here. The objective of step one is to set the ground rules for all of the mapping efforts to follow. In addition to selection of the product family—and therefore the processes that will be mapped—the scope of mapping efforts, roles and responsibilities of those involved, and which general goals should be achieved.

Examining the "future state" of a process also means defining its current state. These future state conceptions can be drawn upon to inform the scope and goal of value stream mapping efforts. In short, a business case must be made for value stream mapping efforts—it is, after all, an expensive and time-consuming process.

In addition to identifying the scope, process boundaries should be identified, as well as differences in value and waste between the current state and the ideal future state. This examination can be classified overall as a design phase, and design tools (such as DMADV) may be applicable for some teams.

When defining boundaries—both the boundaries of the entire process and those of its component steps—a logical starting point is to select points within the process where inputs (raw materials or the work-in-process from the prior workstation) cannot be returned to the previous step. Correctly and satisfactorily defining each step of the process will simplify matters down the road.

Step 2 : Start with the Process Flow

To map the process at its basis, the process flow is first recorded. Every effort should be made to ensure that the process is captured as true to life as possible. This often means doing things the old-fashioned way: with graph paper, a pencil, and a stopwatch.

A good rule of thumb when capturing process data for mapping is to never record information not personally seen. Look at average performance, and rule out clear exceptions that could skew overall interpretation of the process as a whole.

It is important to start with an accurate foundation for this stage and for the stages that follow. It is also important to use a key of standardized icons like the legend pictured below to make the final product truly part of the common language of value stream mapping. If a finished VSM was constructed using icons and flowchart symbols that only the mapping team understood, then each new person who had to interpret the map would need a lesson on which symbols represented what components of the mapped process. A good rule of thumb is to stick to the commonly accepted symbols—but always keep a key handy.

fig. 53

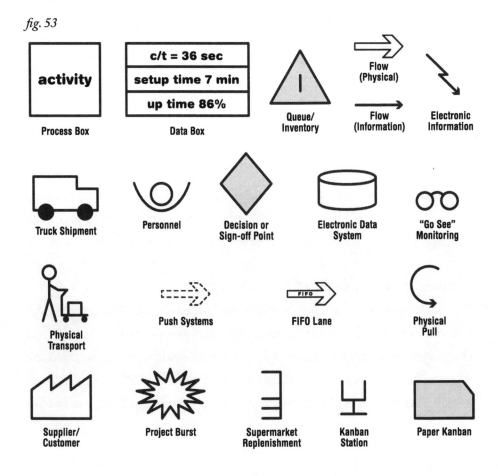

The process map is constructed in the same direction that demand travels through the value stream itself—starting with the customer and working "backward" toward suppliers. To verify that the process has been completely captured, a SIPOC diagram of the process is a useful checklist, both in the process mapping stage and throughout the remaining stages of the VSM construction. Essentially a blank flowchart for the process at hand, the process map stage is pictured below.

fig. 54

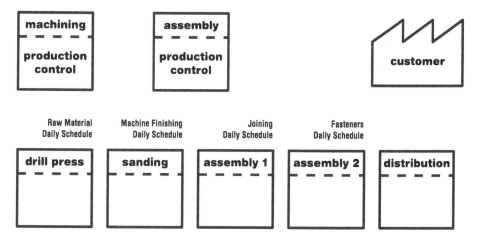

Step 3 : Add the Flow of Materials

The process flow acts as a foundation and basis for the finished value stream map. The material flow step and the following steps are constructed as overlays for the original process map. This fact serves to further underscore the necessity of producing a process map that is an accurate capture of the true-to-life process as it is actually carried out.

Here the flows of all materials are added to the process map. In the case of complex product families with divergent and convergent material flows, group the flows of similar materials together for the sake of simplicity, but don't lose detail in the process. If a material flow is divergent in the actual process, then on the value stream map it should also be represented as such.

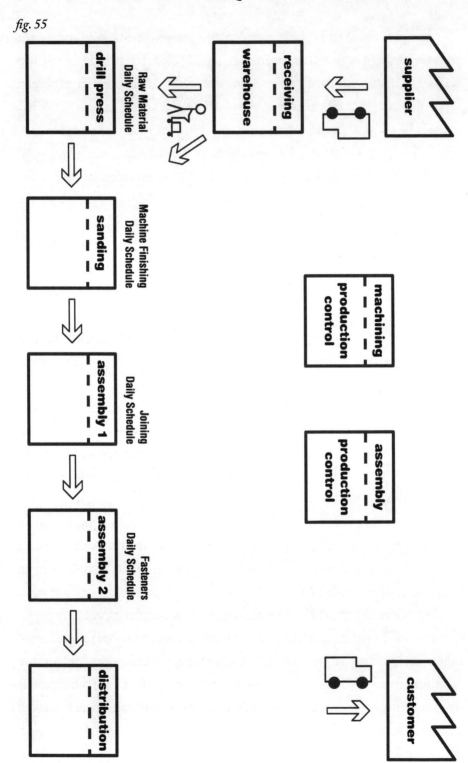

fig. 55

This mapping step also includes the activities that are associated with the flow of materials and interact with it directly; this could include sampling, testing, quality control points, and other analysis measures (see figure 55).

Step 4 : Add the Flow of Information Overlay

Added as another overlay, the visual representation of the flows of information across the value stream is the next component in the mapping process. All forms of communication and information flows are relevant to this mapping stage, but especially the methods by which different elements of the value stream communicate with one another, specifically how the whole process communicates with supplier(s) and customer(s).

Scheduling, scheduling methods, and the way in which they interact with the workstations and flows that they impact are also critical components of the information flow overlay. Despite the fact that the "flow of information" can sometimes be an abstract concept, it can still be mapped, visualized, and analyzed. Activities that meet those three criteria are also visible, and true to Lean, Lean Six Sigma, and the practice of value stream mapping visibility leads to action (see figure 56).

Step 5 : Add Relevant Process Data

Process data is critical to understanding the actual characteristics of flow through the process. The data collected in this stage will inform the next one, so just as with each one of the preceding stages, accuracy and a true-to-life capture of data is of paramount importance.

The specific process data that is relevant to the goals of value stream mapping can vary slightly with decision maker preference, the nature of the process—for example temperature may be a relevant metric for some processes and irrelevant for others—and the complexity of operations.

fig. 56

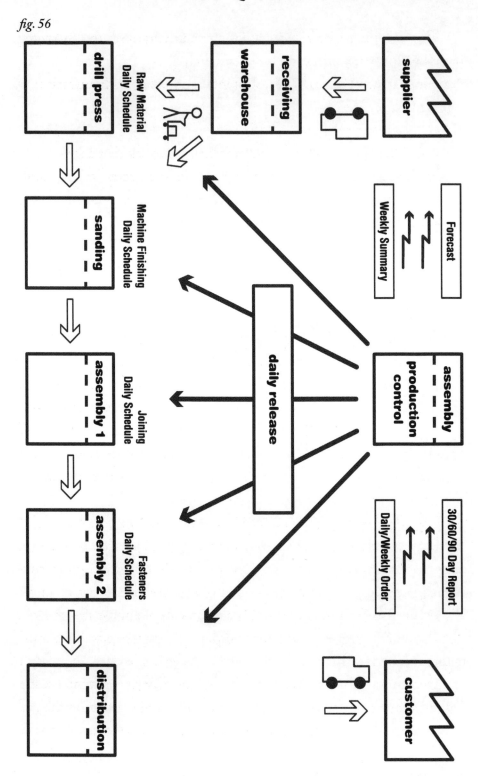

A good rule of thumb is to collect data regarding the following process aspects:

- Trigger (what initiates the step as defined by its boundaries)
- Setup time
- Processing time per unit
- Takt time (this is a measurement of customer demand)
- Scrap rate (the measure of defect rate or defective production)
- Number of people
- Downtime (expressed as a percentage)
- Work-in-progress both down and upstream
- Cost of links (examples include links to the supplier, the warehouse, to IT, et cetera)
- Batch size

Step 6 : Add Process & Lead Time

Lead time has such an outsized impact on business decisions and operations that its importance cannot be overstated. Lead time impacts delivery time, which impacts the creation of value for the customer (late delivery is not valuable) and customer satisfaction. Lead time is a massive factor in scheduling, and controlling lead time is the core of Just-in-Time production and inventory methods.

The most widely accepted convention for recording process and lead time is with the sawtooth timeline (figure 57). Here, production lead time is shown on the "peaks" of the timeline, and the processing time per unit is recorded in the "valleys" of the line. There is, however, no universally accepted standard to this component of a value stream map, and therefore some organizations and decision makers have developed their own methods.

Due to some confusion over the sawtooth-style timelines, some organizations simply use a straight line with lead time listed on the top of the line and process time listed below (with the two values vertically

fig. 57

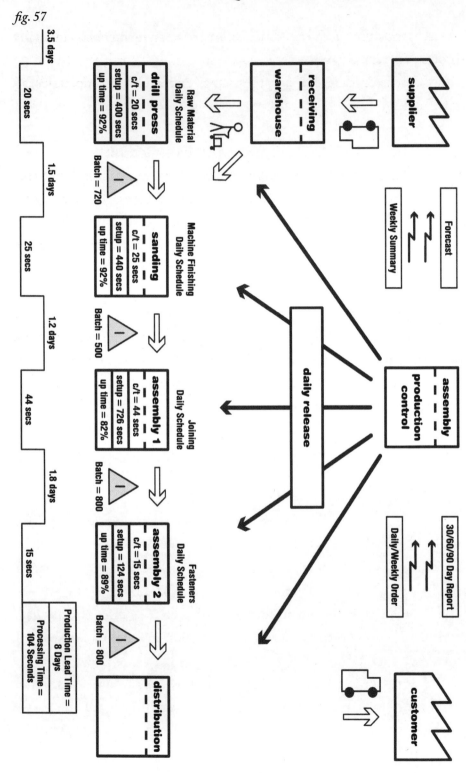

aligned). This prevents potential instances of team members accidentally transposing the two values. Other decision makers have chosen to simply focus on different measures altogether, such as production lead time and VAT (value-added time).

Step 7 : Verify the Map with Non-Familiar Staff

The last step of the value stream mapping process is the independent verification stage. It's a mandatory "extra set of eyes," especially eyes that are not familiar with the process. Here it is absolutely critical that universal value stream mapping symbols have been used, because the test of an effective value stream map is that uninitiated staff can read and correctly draw the appropriate insights from the completed map.

Suppliers and customers should also be consulted, if possible, to ensure that the VSM is as accurate and true to life as possible. If errors are detected in this stage, the problem must be resolved before tactical improvement plans are formulated that rely on the data included in the finished value stream map.

appendix b

fig. 58

defect	week				Total
	1	2	3	4	
Ice Cream Too Soft	xx		x	xxxxx	8
Sprinkles Clumped Together	x	xxxxx	x	xx	9
Soft Serve Machine Jammed	x	x			2
Out of Stock on a Popular Flavor			x		1

Sample Checksheet 1

fig. 59

Completed Calls for Dept. A								Total
week of 6/2 – 6/7								
6/2	X	X	X	X	X	X	X	7
6/3	X	X	X					3
6/4	X	X	X	X				4
6/5	X	X	X	X	X			5
6/6	X							1
6/7	X	X	X	X	X	X	X	7
								27

Sample Checksheet 2

fig. 60

Data Point	xi - x̄	Result²
4	-21.7	472.34
6	-19.7	389.40
7	-18.7	350.94
8	-17.7	314.47
8	-17.7	314.47
14	-11.7	137.67
15	-10.7	115.20
16	-9.7	94.74
17	-8.7	76.27
17	-8.7	76.27
17	-8.7	76.27
21	-4.7	22.40
21	-4.7	22.40
22	-3.7	13.94
23	-2.7	7.47
24	-1.7	3.00
27	1.3	1.60
27	1.3	1.60
29	3.3	10.67
30	4.3	18.20
35	9.3	85.87
36	10.3	105.40
36	10.3	105.40
38	12.3	150.47
39	13.3	176.00
41	15.3	233.07
46	20.3	410.74
49	23.3	541.34
49	23.3	541.34
50	24.3	588.87

Complete Data from Chapter 2 – Six Sigma: Key Tools & Processes, Statistical Analysis, Variation

glossary

5 Whys
A cause and effect investigative tool that consists of a progressive iteration of the question "why?".

5M
The 5 M's of manufacturing. The 5 M's represent the primary categories of causal effects that should be considered when brainstorming potential causes for inclusion in a fishbone diagram. The 5 M's are as follows: machine, method, material, manpower, and measurement.

5S Method
A process-oriented program of workplace organization. The 5S method standardizes best practices for the efficient execution of day-to-day activities. The 5 S's are as follows: sort, segregate, shine, standardize, and self-discipline.

ANOVA
Analysis of Variables. A software-based statistical comparison of two sets of data to identify significant variation. ANOVA analyses identify variation between two sets, but do not identify which elements vary from one another. A Tukey's Pairwise Comparison is often also required to identify specific areas of variation.

Attribute Nominal Data
Discrete datum points that are labels without a relevant order or measurable magnitude. Labels are important aspects of information gathering, but attempting to derive insights from attribute nominal data is useless—they do not represent concrete data within the real world. Example: Dept. A, Dept. B, Dept. C...

Attribute Ordinal Data
Discrete datum points that are labels with relevant order that conforms to an ordinal scale. Attribute ordinal data does not provide a scale or magnitude in the sense that the difference between each of the values is not measurable and the impact of each value is poorly defined. Example: Poor, Satisfactory, Good, Outstanding.

Binary Data
Discrete data that can only be expressed as one of two possible outcomes. Example: Yes/No, Pails/Fail.

Box Plots
Visual representations of data that can be used to quickly compare two data sets and identify outliers. Box plots represent 50% of the data that falls inside the IQR (interquartile range) as a shaded box, then the remaining 50% is displayed outside the box. 1.5x the IQR in either direction is represented by terminating lines known as whiskers. Any outliers are plotted as individual points outside these whiskers.

Checksheets

Organized data collection forms that are designed to simplify and standardize the data collection process. Checksheets should be created specifically for the data collection use at hand to ensure that critical observations are recorded on a consistent basis.

Colored Belt System

The organizational hierarchy prescribed by the Six Sigma program whereby different groups of staff members are identified with colored belts or ranks similar to martial arts programs. These rank assignments reflect that group's involvement in the Six Sigma process.

Continuous Data

Data that can be measured on a continuum scale and can be divided infinitely. Example: call duration, temperature, lead time.

Convenience (Sampling)

Sampling through convenience is considered a poor method of data collection and should be avoided. Simply only gathering sampling data that can be accessed with convenience does not paint an accurate picture and will not represent the population at large.

Count Data

Discrete data that represents physical counts. Example: counted number of defects, counted number of calls.

Critical-to-Quality Requirements

Actionable parameters and specifications that are generated from collected VOC (Voice of the Customer Data). CTQ requirements are the practical application of often vague or poorly defined customer needs.

Customer Segmentation

The process of classifying and organizing different groups of customers based on their value to the organization and other relevant characteristics. Different segments may have different needs, and therefore may generate different CTQ requirements. Example: B2B customers, B2C customers.

D.O.W.N.T.I.M.E.

An acronym that represents the eight sources of waste that make up muda, or physical waste within the Lean system. They are defective production, over-processing, waiting, non-used (or underutilized) employee talent, transportation, inventory, motion, and excessive production.

Defect

Any aspect of a product or service that fails to meet a customer's needs or does not match specifications. This could be defective production or less tangible defects such as failure to deliver within budget, or late delivery.

Descriptive Statistics

Statistical analysis of an entire population, as opposed to inferring attributes of that population via a representative sample (inferential statistics).

Discrete Data

Any data that is not continuous is considered discrete data. Discrete data cannot be measured on a continuum scale, and it cannot be divided infinitely. Discrete data can be broken into four subcategories: count data, binary data, attribute nominal data, and attribute ordinal data.

DMADV

Also known as Design for Six Sigma, DMADV is a structured approach to the design and introduction of new processes and product lines. DMADV is an acronym meaning design, measure, analyze, design, and verify.

DMAIC

A core theme to the Six Sigma and Lean Six Sigma programs, DMAIC is a structured improvement program that aims to improve processes through the use of data collection and analysis methods. DMAIC is an acronym that stands for design, measure, analyze, improve, and control.

DPMO

"Defects per million opportunities" or an expression of a processes' overall defect rate.

Economies of Repetition

The concept that the more frequently a standardized process is completed the higher the degree of accuracy and process adherence is achieved by the staff that performs these activities.

Economies of Scale

The concept that producing larger quantities of goods spreads fixed costs out over a larger number of units therefore decreasing overall cost. This is a common feature of traditional push production systems.

Fishbone Diagram

Also known as an Ishikawa diagram or a herringbone diagram, fishbone diagrams are effective cause and effect tools that can be used to investigate the root causes of unwanted effects.

Inferential Statistics

Statistical analysis of a representative sample instead of an entire population. Inferential methods save data collectors time and increase the speed of the decision making process. The opposite of inferential methods is the practice of descriptive statistics, or the statistical analysis of an entire population at once.

Inputs

Anything that, once processed (run through a process) produces outputs. Inputs can be materials, supplies, effort, administrative duties, or even transportation.

Interquartile Range (IQR)

The IQR is the difference between the upper and lower quartiles. This value is used to identify the upper and lower bounds of a box plot, and the area of 3IQR determines the length of a box plot's whiskers (1.5IQR in each direction). Any values that fall outside of the whiskers are considered outliers.

Ishikawa Diagrams

See Fishbone Diagrams

Judgment (Sampling)

Sampling through judgment—even best judgment—is considered a poor method of data collection and should be avoided. Simply only gathering the data that a collector feels is appropriate will result in biased and inaccurate data.

Just-In-Time
An inventory and production management system that emphasizes speed and flexibility. Just-in-Time methods rely on tight scheduling to ensure that instead of carrying inventories, the materials for production are delivered in time for production and that finished goods are similarly moved downstream within the supply chain—delivered as needed and not kept in inventory.

Kano Analysis
A refining process that aid decision makers in understanding the relationship between customer requirements and deliverables.

Little's Law
A formula used to calculate process lead time which is a component of the PCE (process cycle efficiency) calculation.

Machine (5M)
A causal category for the construction of fishbone diagrams. The machine category encompasses any equipment related to the process at hand. This includes computer systems and production tools primarily, but also extends to all tools that may be a part of the production process.

Manpower (5M)
A causal category for the construction of fishbone diagrams. The manpower category encompasses any people who might have a causal impact on the process at hand.

Material (5M)
A causal category for the construction of fishbone diagrams. The material category encompasses any and all materials that are involved in the production cycle and that may have a causal impact on the process at hand.

Mean
The arithmetical average of a set of data.

Measurement (5M)
A causal category for the construction of fishbone diagrams. The measurement category encompasses any and all measurements and data collection that may occur in regard to the process at hand. This includes the accuracy of observations, thoroughness of investigations, and the calibration of data-gathering equipment.

Measurement Selection Matrix
A visual tool that is used to determine which x and y factors relate to which customer requirements. This tool can be helpful when decision makers are attempting to understand which metrics to measure about a process.

Measures of Central Tendency
The tendency of data to cluster around a central point or value. The three most common measures of central tendency are mean, median, and mode.

Measures of Spread
Calculations that identify the variation within a data set. This includes the range, variance, and standard deviation.

Median
A measure of central tendency, the median is the middle number in an ordered data set.

Method (5M)
A causal category for the construction of fishbone diagrams. The method category encompasses the total sum of protocols, process design, and methodology employed for the execution of the process at hand.

Mode
A measure of central tendency. The mode is the most commonly occurring number in a data set.

Muda
One of the three wastes outlined by the Lean production system. Muda translates from Japanese as "futility," and it represents physical waste.

Mura
One of the three wastes outlined by the Lean production system. Mura represents waste in the form of unevenness.

Muri
One of the three wastes outlined by the Lean production system. Muri represents waste in the form of overburden.

Population Sampling
A component of inferential statistics whereby a representative sample of a population is collected. Insights produced from the analysis of this sample can be inferred to represent the population at large. Sampling and other inferential statistical methods save time during the data collection process and increase the speed of date-informed decisions.

Predictor Measures
Predictor measures are lead measures that can serve as indicators to the outcome of a process. The "inputs" and "process" segments of a business process (x factors) are predictor measures.

Process Cycle Efficiency (PCE)
PCE is a concise measurement of a process' efficiency and performance. It is a measure of "value-add time" compared against the lead time for that same process.

Process Mapping
The visual documentation of a process from start to finish. Process mapping is a flowchart-style representation of a process that has a multitude of uses from internal communication, to external communication, cause and effect investigation, and training. Process mapping is a less involved and less detailed visual aid than the much more complex value stream map.

Process Sampling
Samples taken from a changing or continuous flow. Process sampling can be described as the sampling of every nth unit, or taking a sample at a regular time or cycle intervals.

Product Family Grid
A visual tool that organizes products or services into "families" based on similar components such as shared sub processes or common materials.

Pull Production System

An essential component of the Lean production system, the pull production system is a responsive and flexible manufacturing method that relies on customer demand to "pull" materials through production. Instead of the traditional push production methods of leveraging the economies of scale through large batch sizes and relying on artificial forecasted demand, the pull production system emphasizes meeting the customer's needs through small batch sizes and low-inventory methods such as Just-in-Time.

Push Production

The push production system is a more traditional approach to manufacturing. Utilizing large batch sizes to leverage the economies of scale, push production manufacturers rely on artificial forecasted demand.

Range

A measure of spread, the range of a set of data is the lowest value (min) subtracted from the highest value (max).

Result Measures

Result measures are lag measures that are dependent on predictor measures (lead measures, x factors). Result measures are represented by y factors, and are the outputs of a process.

Segregate (5S)

A component of the 5S system, segregate is the organization of sorted items, tools, and materials into their most useful and efficient layout or configuration so that the necessary tools are always at hand.

Self-Discipline (5S)

A component of the 5S system, the self-disciple element ties all of the 5S activities together by generating the standard for regular application and protocol.

Shine (5S)

A component of the 5S system, the shine element strives to produce a clean and tidy production environment. Clutter creates waste and inefficiency as well as safety hazards. Shine also encompasses the idea of inspection through cleaning, or the regular maintenance of equipment through normal cleaning activities.

SIPOC Diagram

A SIPOC diagram is a snapshot of a process' suppliers, inputs, processes, outputs, and customers presented in the order in which they interact with one another.

Sort (5S)

A component of the 5S system, is an everything-has-a-place approach to a clean, efficient, and clutter free workstation. As an activity, sort strives to identify and reduce the number of items that are unnecessary from specific workstations.

Spaghetti Plots

Also known as workflow diagrams, spaghetti plots are visual diagrams of physical work flow. They present a complete visual picture of how "things" move throughout a process or a space—these "things" could be people, materials, finished goods, or even information and financials.

Standard Deviation

Standard deviation is the average distribution of variation within a data set, or the average distance that each data point is away from the mean. Standard deviation is represented by the Greek letter lower case sigma (σ).

Standardization (5S)

A component of the 5S system, standardization is the process by which the other 5S elements are maintained and regularly applied for best impact.

Stratification Factors

The contributive factors (known as strata) that can segregate groups of data into subgroups. This method of classification can reduce the complexity of difficult-to-handle problems and allow decision makers to investigate root causes in a more effective and comprehensive way.

Total Productive Maintenance (TPM)

An in depth and comprehensive program that strives to reduce downtime due to equipment failure or malfunction. Focusing on preventative and predictive maintenance, TPM is a standardized approach to equipment maintenance and care with a wide range of applications.

Total Quality Management (TQM)

A parallel quality improvement program to Six Sigma that focuses on quality improvement and a customer-centric specification set.

Tukey's Pairwise Comparison

A follow-up computation of the results of an ANOVA analysis. A pairwise comparison compares every data point within the analyzed sets to identify the exact locations of statistical differences; while ANOVA analyses identify statistical differences, they fail to identify the exact location(s) within the compared data sets.

Value Stream Mapping

A complex and costly examination of a process that provides invaluable insight for decision makers. Produced as a series of steps that overlay one another, a complete value stream map includes the total picture of all of the aspects of a process. While the critical value of a value stream map to decision makers cannot be overstated, the process should be reserved for similarly critical and high volume processes due to the labor intensive nature of this visual aid's construction.

Variance

Within the field of statistics, variance is defined as how far away data points are from the mean of the set. Practically speaking, this is the number of units in production that are outside of tolerances.

Voice of the Customer (VOC)

A unifying concept between the Lean and Six Sigma programs, VOC data represents the needs of the customer. Once distilled into actionable goals, this raw data becomes the CTQ requirements that drive the definition and identification if defects, as well as the specifications for production. Voice of the Customer data can be collected in a number of ways, such as interviews, focus groups, point-of-use observations, and surveys. Best when used in conjunction with one another, these methods should be tailored to the customer segment.

Workflow Diagrams

See Spaghetti Plots

answers

Chapter One
1b, 2b, 3d

Chapter Two
1b, 2d, 3b, 4b, 5d, 6c

Chapter Three
1c, 2d, 3b

Chapter Four
1d, 2b, 3b, 4a, 5c, 6d, 7a, 8d

Chapter Five
1b, 2b, 3d, 4b, 5c

about clydebank

We are a multi-media publishing company that provides reliable, high-quality, and easily accessible information to a global customer base. Developed out of the need for beginner-friendly content that can be accessed across multiple platforms, we deliver unbiased, up-to-date, information through our multiple product offerings.

Through our strategic partnerships with some of the world's largest retailers, we are able to simplify the learning process for customers around the world, providing our readers with an authoritative source of information for the subjects that matter to them. Our end-user focused philosophy puts the satisfaction of our customers at the forefront of our mission. We are committed to creating multi-media products that allow our customers to learn what they want, when they want, and how they want.

ClydeBank Business is a division of the multimedia-publishing firm ClydeBank Media. ClydeBank Media's goal is to provide affordable, accessible information to a global market through different forms of media such as eBooks, paperback books and audio books. Company divisions are based on subject matter, each consisting of a dedicated team of researchers, writers, editors and designers.

For more information, please visit us at :
www.clydebankmedia.com
or contact info@clydebankmedia.com

Your world. simplified.

notes

STAY INFORMED

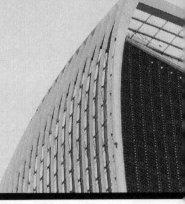

ClydeBank BUSINESS | BLOG

Your Source for All Things Business

Why Should I Sign Up for the Mailing List?

- Get a $10 ClydeBank Media gift card!
- Be the first to know about new products
- Receive exclusive promotions & discounts

Stay on top of the latest business trends by joining our free mailing list today at:

www.clydebankmedia.com/business-blog

Made in the USA
Lexington, KY
09 August 2018